S0-BBE-344

LAST TALKS AT SAANEN
1985

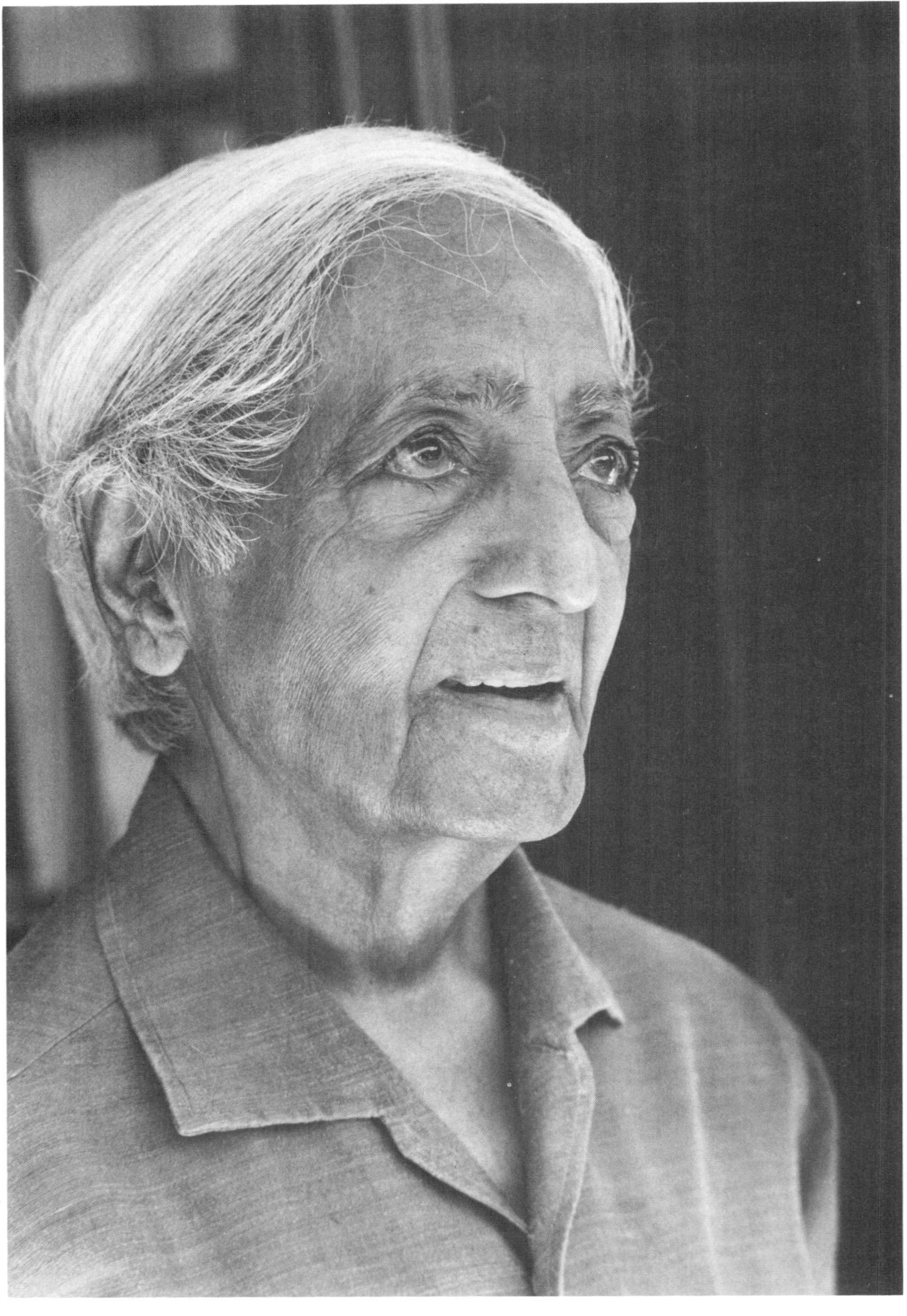

LAST TALKS AT SAANEN 1985

by

J. KRISHNAMURTI

Photographs by Mark Edwards

HARPER & ROW, PUBLISHERS, SAN FRANCISCO

Cambridge, Hagerstown, New York, Philadelphia, Washington
London, Mexico City, São Paulo, Singapore, Sydney

BY J. KRISHNAMURTI

The Awakening of Intelligence
Beyond Violence
Education and the Significance of Life
The Ending of Time (with David Bohm)
Exploration into Insight
First and Last Freedom
The Flame of Attention
The Flight of the Eagle
Freedom from the Known
The Future of Humanity (with David Bohm)
Krishnamurti on Education
Krishnamurti's Journal
Krishnamurti's Notebook
Life Ahead
The Network of Thought
Think On These Things
Truth and Actuality: *Conversations on Science and Consciousness*
The Wholeness of Life
You Are the World

Frontispiece: Krishnamurti at Rougemont near Saanen looking at the mountains

 For information address Harper & Row, Publishers, Inc., 10 East 53rd Street, New York, NY 10022. Published simultaneously in Canada by Fitzhenry & Whiteside, Limited, Toronto.

FIRST U.S. EDITION

Library of Congress Cataloging-in-Publication Data
Krishnamurti, J. (Jiddu)
Last talks at Saanen, 1985.
I. Title.
B5134.K753L37 1987 181′.4 86-45814
ISBN 0-06-064798-1

87 88 89 90 91 RRD 10 9 8 7 6 5 4 3 2 1

CONTENTS

FOREWORD

This book is a commemoration of Krishnamurti's last talks at Saanen, Switzerland, after twenty-five years of holding international summer gatherings there. It was a lucky coincidence that Mark Edwards was at Saanen that summer to photograph the gathering from the beginning, for Krishnamurti's decision to hold no more talks there was not announced until almost the end of the meetings. Krishnamurti's reason for giving up the Saanen gatherings was that at ninety he felt he should somewhat curtail his travelling.

Saanen is a pretty little village in the Bernese Oberland which Krishnamurti had first seen when he went in 1957 to stay with a friend at the neighbouring town of Gstaad. He already knew Switzerland well, however, from the many visits he had made to Villars throughout the years. He had always loved mountains and mountain scenery.

In 1961 an Italian friend rented for him for the summer a furnished house at Gstaad, Chalet Tannegg, and for the next twenty-three years he spent several weeks at this same villa, rented each summer. (It was only in the last two years, after Tannegg was sold, that he had to find other accommodation near Saanen.) He always arrived at Tannegg well before the talks began and remained there for some time afterwards.

During the first summer of 1961, a small gathering was arranged for him at the Landhaus in Saanen (the Town Hall) which held only about 350 people; nevertheless, nineteen different nationalities were represented at the talks he gave there. Aldous Huxley, a great friend whom Krishnamurti had first met in California, happened to be at Gstaad that summer and went several times to hear him speak. Describing the talk of August 6, Huxley wrote: '. . . it was among the most impressive things I have ever heard. It was like listening to a discourse of the Buddha—such power, such intrinsic authority, such an uncompromising refusal to allow the *homme moyen sensuel* any *gurus*, saviours, führers, churches. "I show you sorrow and the ending of sorrow"—and if you don't choose to fulfil the conditions for ending sorrow, be prepared, whatever gurus, churches etc. you may believe in, for the continuation of sorrow.'

The following year a much larger gathering was held in a tent with a geodesic dome, invented by Buckminster Fuller, the architect-designer, famous in America. It was erected on the Saanen air-strip.

In 1963 the same tent was put up on the only completely flat land at Saanen, apart from the air-strip, that had not been built over. The river Saane flows beside this site of 1¾ acres and there are woods on two sides. This land was bought in 1965 with funds contributed to Krishnamurti's work, and administered by a legally constituted committee. Thereafter all the gatherings took place on this site. In 1968 the domed tent, then worn out, was replaced, and there has since been only one other replacement.

The attendance at these Saanen gatherings increased every year. At the last gathering more than 3,000 people crowded into the tent for the five talks and three Question and Answer meetings given by Krishnamurti. Almost every nationality, a huge variety of types and a wide range of ages were represented. Some people went merely for the day; many more stayed for the whole gathering. Caravans and campers were accommodated in the municipal camping site; others rented chalets or stayed in hotels or guest houses in Saanen itself or in neighbouring villages. Some, who could not afford the guest houses, slept in dormitories, either in the old disused schoolhouse or in buildings occasionally used by the military. Those who wanted it were provided with one hot meal a day at minimal cost, cooked in an improvised kitchen and eaten out of doors.

The gatherings could never have taken place if it had not been for the unstinted voluntary help given by so many in the course of those twenty-five years. At the last few gatherings the talks were recorded on tape and also on video. The tapes were immediately transcribed and copies given to the translators who superimposed the translations on to the video tapes, on a parallel track, as well as recording them on audio tape. Thus on the following day not only were the video tapes and cassettes of the previous day's talk on sale in English, German, French, Italian, Dutch and Spanish, but video showings were given in those same languages.

The last Saanen gathering of 1985 was blessed with a spell

of really beautiful weather. At the first Question and Answer meeting, after it had been publicly announced that this was to be the last gathering, Krishnamurti began his address characteristically: 'I am told that there are so many people who are sad leaving, ending Saanen. If one is sad it is about time that we left.'

But at his last meeting he spoke with great feeling: 'We have had the most marvellous days, lovely mornings, beautiful evenings, long shadows and deep blue valleys and clear blue sky and the snow. A whole summer has never been like this. So the mountains, the valleys, the trees and the river, tell us goodbye.'

Previous page: Saanen valley. Tent is hidden behind long avenue of trees to the right of the picture

Facing page: Krishnamurti on his favourite walk near Gstaad

Above: Chalet Tannegg, Gstaad, where Krishnamurti stayed

Transporte
BIGLEN

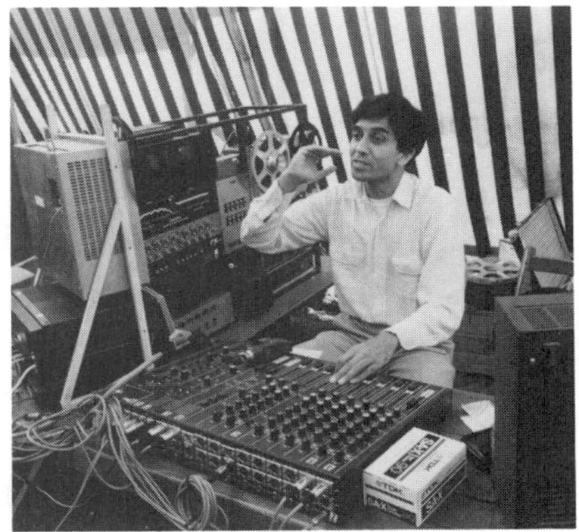

Facing page:
Top: Preparing the tent for the talks

Middle: Placing water pipes over tent for cooling

Bottom: Bringing in benches for the audience

Above left: Setting up video equipment in a van

Below left: Setting out video cassettes and books for sale

Above right: Adjusting audio equipment

Above: Camping for the talks

Facing page:
Top and middle: Preparing an inexpensive meal

Bottom: Eating the meal by the river Saane

Sunbathing in the mountains above Saanen

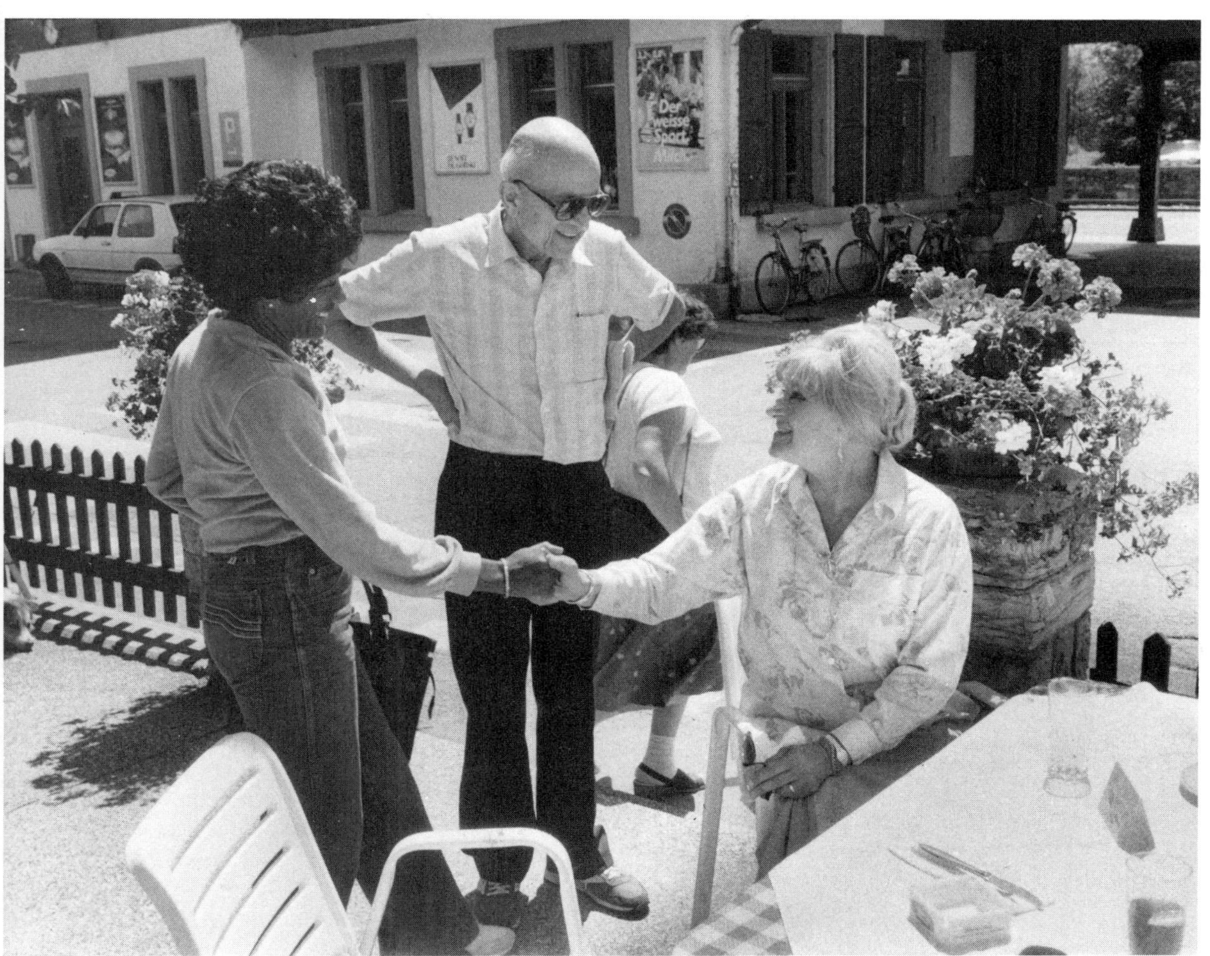

Meeting at the Saanerhof Hotel before a talk

Queuing for a talk

Krishnamurti arriving for a Question and Answer meeting carrying the questions

Left: Entering the tent

Following pages:

Top left: Transcribing a talk

Middle left: Making audio cassettes of the talks for sale

Bottom left: Books, audio cassettes and video cassettes being sold in the tent after a talk

Right: The French translation of a talk

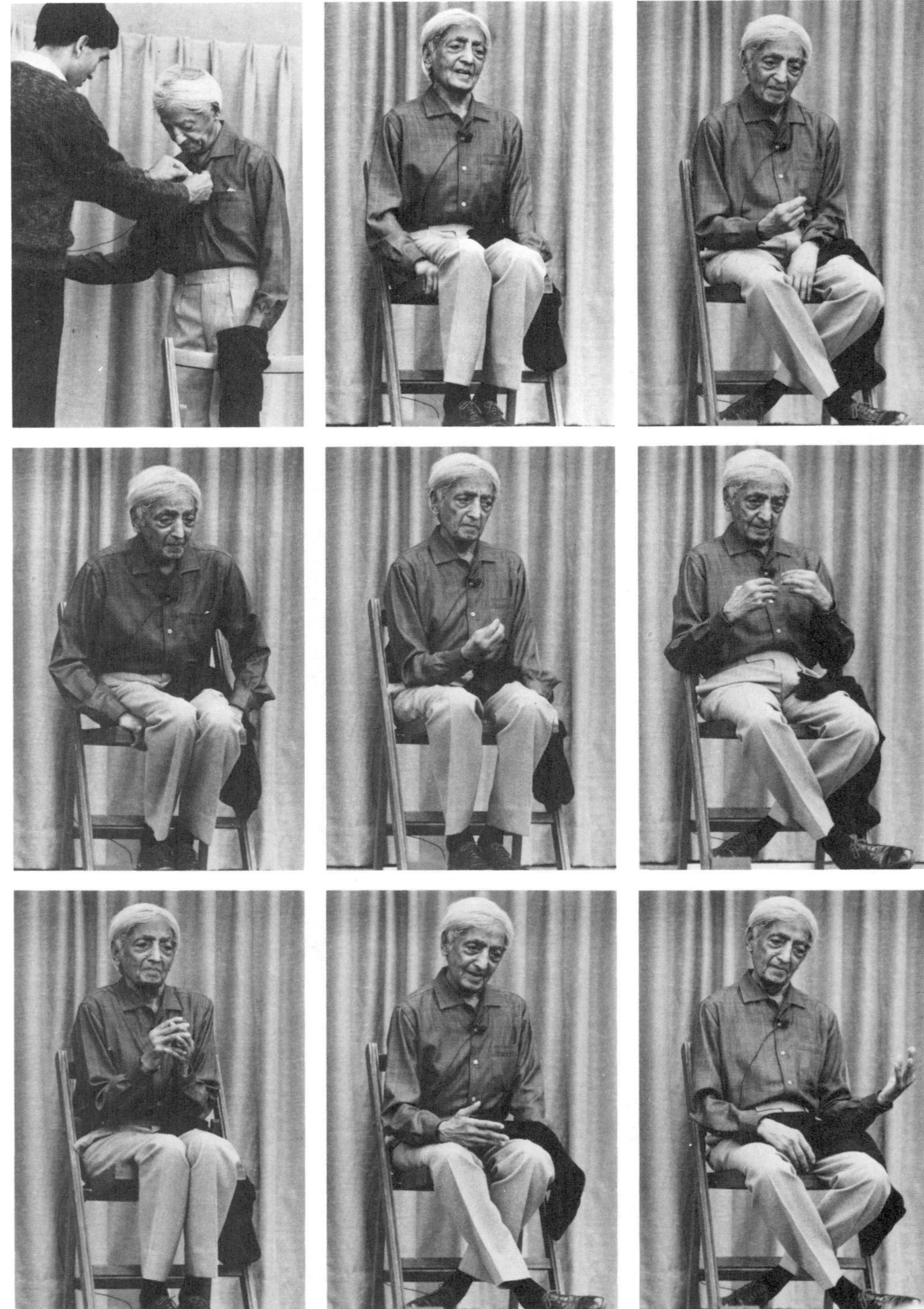

TALK ONE
SUNDAY, JULY 7

If one may, one would like to point out that we are a gathering of serious people who are concerned with daily life. We are not concerned whatsoever with beliefs, ideologies, suppositions, theoretical conclusions or theological concepts, nor are we trying to found a sect, a group of people who follow somebody. We are not, let's hope, frivolous but rather we are concerned together with what is happening in the world—all the tragedies, the utter misery, poverty—and our responsibility to it.

One would also like to point out, if one may, that you and I, the speaker, are walking, taking a journey, together, not in an aeroplane high up at 30,000 or 40,000 feet, but walking along a quiet road, a long endless road all over the world where one sees appalling terrorism, the killing of people for no purpose, threatening people, kidnapping them, highjacking, murdering, wars. We don't seem to care very much. It is only when it happens very close to us that we become concerned, worried, fearful. When it is far away from us, we are more indifferent.

This is what is happening in the world—economic division, religious division, political division and all the religious, sectarian divisions. There is a great deal of danger, hazard. One doesn't know what is going to happen in the future, not only in our own lifetime but in our children's and grandchildren's. The whole world is in a great state of crisis and the crisis is not only out there but also in each one of us. If you are at all aware of all this, what is the responsibility for it on the part of each one of us? One must have asked this question of oneself very often: what is one to do? Where should one begin? What should each one of us do, facing this terrible society in which we live, each concerned with himself, with his own fulfilment, with his own sorrow, with his own misery, economic struggle, and so on and so on? Each one of us is concerned with himself. What shall we do? Shall we pray to God—repeat prayers over and over and over again? Or belong to some sect, follow some guru, escape from the world, put on some medieval dress or modern robes of a peculiar colour? Can we withdraw from the world at all, like monks?

Seeing all this, observing it intimately—not as something you have read about in the newspapers, or been told about by journalists, novels, television—what is the role of each one of us, the responsibility?

As we said, we are not trying to entertain you, or trying to tell you what you should do—what each one of us should do. We have had leaders galore, political, economic, religious, sectarian, and they have been *utterly* helpless, they have their own theories, their own way, and there are thousands of people who are following them, all over the world. They have really enormous wealth, not only the wealth of the Roman Catholic Church but also the wealth of the gurus. It all ends up in money.

So, if one may ask: what shall we do together? Or what shall we do as a single human being? Are we at all concerned, or are we seeking some peculiar satisfaction, gratification for ourselves? Are we committed to a certain symbol, religious or otherwise, and clinging to that, hoping that what lies behind that symbol will help us? This is a very serious question. It is becoming much more serious now, for there is the threat of war and then total uncertainty.

May I, may the speaker, inform you of a conversation he had with a Mr X which continued for several days? Mr X has travelled all over the world, more or less, he told the speaker. He is fairly well read, has been to various institutions, sometimes joining them, and with a rush getting out of them. He followed one guru or another and gave them up. And for a few weeks he tried to become a monk, and that too he gave up. And he looked at the various political parties, at the whole spectrum of political activities, and at last he said, 'I have come to talk with you. I would like to have a conversation with you, at the same level as I am, not that you are pretentious. I don't know your real position or what you are, though I have read something about you.' May I go on with this conversation? Does it interest you?

And he said, 'Let's talk things over together like two friends, you and I—like two friends who have lived together in the world, been through every kind of travail. What is it all about? Why is man born like this? Why has he become after many, many, many millennia what he is now—suffering, anxious, lonely, despairing, with disease, death and always the gods somewhere about? Let's forget all about those gods and talk together as two human beings, living in this world, in this marvellous country, on the earth which is so beautiful, which is the mother of all things.'

And so this Mr X gave something of his inward thoughts, his outward activities. And he said, 'What is all this about? Why are human beings, who are sophisticated, have educated themselves, who have become experts in technology and can argue the hind legs off a donkey, who can invent gods and goddesses and everything—why are human beings all over the world in perpetual conflict—not only with the environment, not only with their governments whom they have elected, or with some dogma invented by ancient priests? Why does each human being everlastingly, from the moment he is born till he dies, live in this conflict?' This was the first question he asked, this Mr X. Why? What is the cause of this conflict, not only outwardly but also most deeply, inwardly, subjectively, inside the skin as it were—why is he in conflict?

Centuries before Christianity, the religions have talked endlessly about peace—be peaceful, be quiet, be gentle, generous, affectionate, loving. In spite of their propaganda this conflict goes on. Is there an answer to this question, a final, irrefutable answer? That is, can human beings in this world, living their daily life, going to the office, keeping a house, sex, children and all that, and also with this search, this longing for something much more than the mere material things of life—can they cease from conflict? Can this question ever be solved? Apparently man has not solved it, though he has lived on this earth for so many million years as a human being.

'We have gathered tremendous experience,' Mr X was telling the speaker. 'We have gathered a great deal of knowledge; we have gathered an immense amount of information technologically, but inwardly we remain barbarians, trying to kill each other, trying to compete with each other, to destroy each other.'

So Mr X came all that way, a long distance by bus, train, aeroplane, and he said, 'Answer this question: is there a cause for this conflict? And if there is a cause then let's discover what the cause is. Not that you are going to lead me or that you will tell me and I will accept, or that I will go and think about it and come to some kind of conclusion of my own, but rather together as two human beings—not one sitting on a platform and the other sitting down below—but together as two human beings who have gone through a great deal of life, the loneliness, the desperation, the anxiety, the uncertainty, wanting love and not finding it, or loving and not being satisfied with that, always pushing, pushing, pushing, always wanting to achieve something, whether it is heaven or illumination or enlightenment or to become a multi-millionaire, which is more or less the same thing, never content, never knowing what peace is, never sitting quietly under a tree looking at the mountains, the rivers, the blade of grass and the beauty of the earth and sunlight, and the glory of an early morning—two human beings asking if there is a cause of this conflict.'

So Mr X said to the speaker, 'Let's talk, let us question

each other, never accepting what the other says. I won't accept a *thing* from you, nor will you accept a *thing* from me. We are on the same level. You may be very clever, you may have a reputation which is nonsense, you may go round the earth, or a certain part of the earth, all that doesn't count. It has no value.' With which the speaker agreed wholeheartedly. 'So let us explore this curse which man has borne from the beginning of time: why man, which includes woman please, lives this way; why man is in conflict in his own intimate relationships, sexually, in a family—the whole network of conflict.'

So Mr X came again the next day, and we continued. We sat on the veranda on a beautiful day overlooking the valley with the great mountains round us, snowcapped, marvellous valleys, blue and lovely azure skies, and the sun glittering on the leaves, the dappled earth. Everything seemed so marvellously alive, pulsating, full of energy. There we were, he and the speaker, watching this great beauty and never being with the beauty, always watching it, never feeling the beauty with one's heart and mind, never being utterly sensitive to all the glory of the earth. He said, 'We won't talk about beauty, this is your business, you tell me about it.' The speaker said he would a little later. 'First let us explore together this question of conflict. We are asking: must human beings bear with it, get accustomed to it, hold it, never, never be able to put it *completely* aside, so that their brains can function as they should, *completely* untethered, *completely* free, not programmed, not conditioned?'

So now the speaker is putting this question to you. And

we also discussed, talked over, debated this point: what is the cause of it? We are taking a journey together, not my asking you to tell me, or I telling you. What is the cause of it? *Everywhere* there is struggle. You might say there is struggle in nature, the big animal lives on the smaller animal and so on. In a forest the little tree is struggling against the gigantic trees for light. You might say everywhere on earth, in nature, there is conflict, some kind of struggle going on, so why shouldn't we also go on in that way because we are part of nature? What human beings call conflict, may not be conflict out there; it may be the most natural way for nature to act: the hawk, the eagle kill the rabbit, bears kill salmon, the tiger kills something swiftly, or the cheetah; in nature killing, killing, killing goes on, and one might say that we are part of nature so it is inevitable that we should be in constant struggle. If one accepts that it is natural, inevitable, there is nothing more to be said about, it; if we say it is natural, we will go on in that way because we are part of the whole earth, but if one begins to question it then where are you? Are you willing together to find out because we are supposed to be a little more active, intelligent than the trees, the tigers, the elephants (fortunately the elephants don't kill too many things, but they destroy trees).

So, if we do not accept that conflict is the way of life, then what is one to do? Where does one start to understand the whole movement of conflict? How does one feel one's way into all this? One way, the speaker said to Mr X, is to analyse very carefully all the factors of conflict, one after the other —through self-analysis or being analysed by another, or accepting the advice of professors, philosophers, psychologists. But will analysis bring about the discovery of the cause, though it may bring you certain intellectual conclusions, or you may put all the analytical factors together and see the whole? Is that possible? Or is there a different approach to the question?

I wonder if Mr X understands what the speaker is saying? The speaker is telling Mr X that analysis implies one who is the analyser—right? Therefore there is an analyser and the analysed, the subject and the object. Is there such a difference in oneself as the subject and the object? That is a question the speaker asks Mr X. You are Mr X. The analyser has been encouraged through education, through conditioning, through being programmed, to believe that he, the analyser, is completely different from that which he analyses, but the speaker says, 'I am going to question this whole attitude towards analysis.' The speaker says, 'I am not accepting what the professionals, including those people who come from Vienna, or the latest American psychologists, say about analysis.' The speaker tells Mr X, 'I am not accepting any of those. I question it; I question not only the activity of analysis but who is the analyser. If you can understand the analyser first then what need is there for analysis?' You understand, sir? Am I going too fast? May we go together into this?

I analyse myself. I have been angry, or greedy, or sexual, whatever it is, and in analysing it, that is, breaking it up and looking at it very carefully step by step, who is the observer? Is not the observer, the analyser, all the accumulated past remembrances? He is conditioned through experience, through his knowledge, his way of looking at life, his peculiar tendencies, his prejudices, his religious programming: all this is the past, all this is the background of his life, from childhood. *He* is the observer, *he* is the analyser, whether or not that background includes communal remembrance, racial remembrance, racial consciousness, *he* is the *observer.* And then the observer breaks it up into the observed and the observer, so that very division in analysis creates conflict. Are we together? You are Mr X, I am the speaker. Are we taking the same journey together? The speaker says that the moment there is a division between the analyser and the analysed there must inevitably be conflict of some kind, subtle, fatuous, without meaning, but it is a conflict—to overcome, conquer, suppress, transcend—all these are efforts in minor or major form.

So one discovers that where there is division between the Swiss and the Germans, the French and the English, I and you, we and they—wherever there is division there must be conflict. Not that there is not division; the rich are very powerful. But if we create subjectively a division—I belong to this and you belong to that, I am a Catholic, you are a Protestant, I am a Jew and you are an Arab—then there is conflict.

So wherever there is division between two people, between man and woman, between God and earth, between 'what should be' and 'what is'—I wonder if Mr X is following all this, not only verbally, intellectually, which is meaningless, but with his heart, with his being, with his vitality, energy and passion—wherever there is division there is conflict.

So one begins to discover the root of conflict. Is it possible for a human being living in a modern world, going to a job, earning a livelihood, business there, family here, aggressive in business and submissive to his wife—is it possible for him to live so that his life does not become a contradiction? Can that contradiction end? If not one will live in conflict, one becomes a hypocrite. If one likes to be a hypocrite, that is all right too, but if one wants to live very honestly, which is *absolutely necessary*, to live with great austere honesty, not to someone, not to one's country, not to one's ideal, but to say *exactly* what one means and mean what one says, not what others have said and which you repeat, or believe in something and do quite the opposite, that is not honesty—if one wants to live very honestly there can be no contradiction.

Everyone talks about peace. Every government, every religion, and every preacher, including the speaker, talks about peace. And to live peacefully demands *tremendous* honesty and intelligence. So is it possible, living in the twentieth century, to live inwardly first, psychologically first, subjectively, and not have in oneself any kind of division? Please do enquire, search, ask with *passion*. Passion doesn't include fanaticism, passion doesn't demand martyrdom. It is not something you are so attached to that that very attachment gives you passion—you understand? That is not passion, it is being tied to something which gives you the feeling of passion, energy, like a donkey tied to a post; it can wander round and round and round but it is still held there.

So could we, Mr X and the speaker, not telling each other what they should do, discover for themselves in all honesty, without any sense of deception, without any sense of illusion, whether it is possible to live in this world—in which you know all the horrors that are going on—without conflict, without division? Don't go to sleep, please, it is too early in the morning. If you are asked—you are Mr X—what would your answer be inwardly? If you are a Swiss, a Hindu, a Muslim, or follow some clique, or some group, or are the follower of some guru wouldn't you have to abandon all that completely? You may have a Swiss passport (the speaker has an Indian passport but he is *not* an Indian—they don't like that in India but we have told them several times not to belong to any cult, to any guru, to anything)—you are going to find this terribly difficult. At the end of it you stand alone, but there is the comprehension, the inward awareness, insight, into all that which is really nonsensical. Belonging to something, belonging to a group, belonging to some sect, may give one momentary satisfaction but that is all becoming rather weary, wretched and ugly.

So can one not be attached to any of this—especially including what the speaker is saying? Strangely, your brain, though not the brain of another, is also the other—you understand? Your brain is like the brain of every other human being. It has *immense* capacity, *immense* energy. Look what they have done in the technological world. All the scientists in America are now concerned with Star Wars. We won't go into all that. The brain has this *extraordinary* energy if you concentrate on something, give your attention to something. They have given attention to killing other human beings, so the atom bomb came into being. Our brains are not ours, they have evolved through a long period of time, and in that evolution we have gathered tremendous knowledge, experience, but in all that there is very little of what is called love. I may love my wife, or my children, or my country. My country has been divided by thought, geographically, but it is the world. The world in which one lives is the entire world. So my brain which has evolved through a long period of time, that brain with its consciousness is not mine because my consciousness is shared with every other human being.

Mr X is saying, 'I have read something about what you have said, I am not repeating what you have said, but this is what I also feel. I see, wherever I have been, in every corner of the earth, that there are human beings who suffer pain, anxiety, desperate loneliness, and so our consciousness is shared by all other human beings.' Do you realize this—not intellectually but actually? If one really feels this, then there will be no division. I ask Mr X, 'Do you see this reality, not a concept of it, not an idea of it, not the beautiful conclusion but the actuality of it? The actuality is different from the idea of actuality—right? You are sitting there, that is actual, but I can imagine that you are sitting there which is totally different.'

So, our brain, which is the centre of our consciousness, with all the nervous responses, sensory responses, the centre of all our knowledge, all our experience, all our memory (your memory may be from another, but it is still memory; you may be highly educated, the other may have no education at all, may not even know how to read and write, but it is still part of the whole)—so your consciousness is shared by every human being on this earth. Therefore you are entire humanity. Do you understand, sirs? You are in *actuality*, not theoretically or theologically, or in the eyes of God—probably gods have no eyes!—but in *actuality* there is this strange irrevocable fact that we all go through the same mould, the same anxiety, hope, fear, death, loneliness that brings such desperation. So we are mankind. And when one realizes *that deeply*, conflict with another ceases because you are like me.

So that is what we talked about, Mr X and Mr K. And we also continued about other things, for he was there for several days. But we first established a real relationship which is so necessary when there is any kind of debate, any kind of communication, not only verbal, for words don't convey profoundly what one desires to convey. So, at the end of the second day, we said, where are we? You, Mr X and Mr K, where are we in this? Have we brought about, not change, change implies time (we will go into that another time)—or have we merely gathered as we gather the harvest? We sow—that is, you have come here, which is part of sowing, and you have listened to K and Mr X—what have you gathered? Gathering means accumulation. You have gathered so much information—please follow this, we will stop presently, don't get sleepy or nervous. You have gathered so much information from professionals, from psychologists, from psychiatrists—gathered, gathered, gathered. The brain is like a magnet, gathering. And K asks Mr X, 'Have you gathered also? If you have gathered then this becomes like any other meeting.' So K asks Mr X, 'What have you gathered? Or are you free from gathering?' Please, if you have the patience, listen to this.

Do we ever stop gathering? For practical things in life one has to gather, but to see where gathering is *not* necessary, that is where the art of living comes. Because if we are gathering, our brain is never free, is never empty—we won't go into the question of emptiness because that is a different matter—but are we aware that we are gathering, gathering, gathering as we gather habits? And when you have gathered so much it is very difficult to get rid of it. This gathering conditions the brain. Born in India, belonging to a certain type of people, tradition, religious, or very, very orthodox, you have gathered all that. And then to be free of all that takes immense enquiry, searching, looking, watching, awareness. So is it possible not to gather at all? Please consider this, don't reject it. Find out. You have to gather knowledge to go to your house, to drive a car, to speak a foreign language, but inwardly is it necessary to gather at all? Enlightenment is *not* gathering. On the contrary it is total freedom from all that. Which is, after all, love, isn't it? I don't love you because I have gathered you. I have been sexually satisfied with you, or you are companionable, or I am lonely and therefore I depend on you; then that becomes a marketable thing; then we exploit each other, use each other, sell each other down the river. Surely that is not love, is it? Love is the quality of a brain that doesn't gather anything at all, and then what it says will be what it has discovered, not what other people have said. And in that there is *tremendous passion*, not lust, passion. But it is not fanaticism. I don't suddenly become a strict vegetarian or won't touch salt. The fanatics all have passion of a certain type but they have become violent, inclined to martyrdom, and all the rest of that business.

So, the speaker, K, is asking Mr X to find out if you can live without gathering. You can't be told about it. We can enquire into it together, but the actuality of never gathering, the accumulated memory never operating, is really very subtle; it requires a great deal of enquiry.

May we stop now? We have talked for an hour. You haven't talked but K has talked. We have established the basis of a communication with each other in which there is no superior and no inferior, one who knows and one who does not know.

TALK TWO
WEDNESDAY, JULY 10

May we continue with what we were talking about the other day? I think it is important to realize that this is not a personality cult. The person called K is not important at all. What is important is what he is saying, not what he looks like, his personality, and all the rest of that nonsense. So please, if one may point out carefully and definitely, the person who is speaking on the platform is in no way important.

We talked the other day about various forms of conflict, what is the cause of it, why throughout the history of mankind, man, including of course woman, has lived in conflict and never solved that problem at all. Throughout the ages, during this long period of evolution, of many, many millennia, we are still in conflict with each other—conflict between man and woman, between human beings, between a group of people, between nations, sexes, religions. I am sure one is aware of all this. The terrorism, the brutality, the appalling cruelty, all the hideous things that are taking place in the world—who is responsible for all this? As we said the other day, this is a serious gathering, not just spending a good morning under a tent or listening to somebody; this is a serious, active, co-operative, definite gathering.

We are asking this morning, who is responsible for all this? Responsibility implies care, attention, not only to what is taking place outwardly in the world, but also inwardly in all of us: who is responsible for this? Are the politicians responsible? That is, let them do what they want to do because we have elected them in a so-called Democratic society. In the Totalitarian states they are not elected, they just come to power and dominate the whole. So who is responsible? The religions? The Islamic world? The Christian world? The Hindu world? Buddhist and so on? Or are we responsible, each one of us? Please do consider this. Is each one of us, living in this world, in this environment, not only in lovely Switzerland but also all over the world, is each one of us—you sitting there, and the speaker here—are we responsible for all this?

I hope you are putting this question to yourself—are you responsible for creating this appalling, dangerous world, brutal and terrifying world? If you have gone to various countries you see all this, enormous poverty, millions upon millions of poor people, starving, and those who are terribly rich, born to high position and for the rest of their lives keeping their riches, castles, mansions and so on. Who is responsible? Are we responsible for creating this society around us, the culture, the religion, the gods, all the rest of that ritualistic repetition and sensation, because we are angry, greedy, violent, disorderly, hating and only limiting our affection to a very, very, very few—has each one of us created this society in which we live? Is that so? Is each one of us responsible? You say, 'I am sorry, I am not', or you may be indifferent to the whole thing as long as you are safe in a particular country, protected by frontiers.

So, we come to a very serious question: what is order and what is disorder? Please, we are discussing, going together into this question. It is not that you will accept, or in any way acquiesce in what the speaker is saying, that would be utterly futile, but could we together take a very long journey, not only intellectually, verbally, but much more profoundly to discover why the society for which we are responsible is creating such terrible disorder and cruelty? Are we different from society, the thing we have created? Must there not be order first in our house—not only in the outer walls of the house and garden, but also in the inward world in which we all live, the subjective world, the psychological world? Is there disorder there? You understand my question? I hope the speaker is making it quite clear. As long as we live, each one of us, in disorder, psychologically, subjectively, inwardly, whatever we do will create disorder. The Totalitarian states have said that by changing society, the environment, forcing it, compelling it, they will change humanity, the human brain. They have not succeeded. There is constant dissent, revolt and all the rest of it.

So, if you see this, that we have created this disorder, and this disorder is the society in which we live, then what shall we do? Where do you start? Do you want to change society as the social reformers do, the do-gooders, the men who want to alter laws, through terrorism, through compulsion? Or do you put your own house inwardly in order? Is the question clear?

So, how shall I, or you, put our house in order? Because that is the only place I can start, not by outward reform, outward change of laws, forming United Nations. If I may digress a little bit, we were invited to speak at the United Nations last year and this year. One of their big shots got up after K had spoken and said, 'At last after forty years of working in this institution, very hard, I have come to the conclusion that we must not kill each other.' Forty years! And we are the same, hoping something will happen out there, something that will compel us, force us, persuade us, drive us. We have depended on the outer—outer challenges, outer wars and so on.

So, what shall we do? It is no good joining little communities, following some guru. That is total irresponsibility. Giving, surrendering, oneself to somebody who calls himself enlightened, leads you to . . . whatever he will lead you to, generally money—so how shall we start inwardly to bring about order? Order implies no conflict, doesn't it? No conflict in oneself, completely no conflict? We went into that question the other day, what is the cause of conflict? Volumes have been written about it. Psychologists, psychiatrists, therapeutists and so on have explained verbally; millions of words have been spilled over it, and yet we remain, all of us, in conflict. Where the mind, the brain is in disorder, which is the essence of conflict, that brain can never be orderly, simple, clear. That can be taken for granted as a law, like the law of gravity, the law that the sun rises in the east and sets in the west: where there is subjective or inward conflict there must be disorder. Look into it, please, carefully.

And what is the nature of disorder? Not what is order, because a confused mind can invent order and say, 'That is order.' A brain that is caught in illusions, as most people's are, will create its own order out of confusion—right? So, what is the nature of disorder? Why do we say there must be order and then be in disorder? Why do we separate the two? We say we realize that we are in disorder, which is fairly simple, and then we are seeking order out of that. The politicians know there is disorder and they are seeking order. Is this clear? Of course. Not only the politicians but each one of us knows that our life is in disorder. Going to the office in the morning from nine till five—what a life you lead!—struggling, fighting, ambitious, greedy, aggressive, climbing the ladder and then coming home and being very docile, submitting to your wife, or husband, or whoever it is. There is disorder in this, and all the time the brain is seeking order —all the time—because it cannot live in disorder; it cannot function clearly, beautifully, exquisitely, to its highest capacity when there is disorder. Therefore there is a slight search for order in all of us. So we are asking: why is there this division—wanting order and then living in disorder? I don't know if you are following all this. Don't be puzzled, it is very simple.

We live in disorder, that is certain. Why bother about order? Let us see if we can clear up disorder. If you can clear it up then there is order. There is not this conflict between disorder and order. Look: it is fairly simple this. We are violent people, aggressive, not only physically but also psychologically, inwardly. We want to hurt people. We say things brutally about others. Violence is not merely physical action; violence is also psychological—aggressive, imitative, comparing oneself with another and so on, all that is a form of violence. We are, by nature from the animal, violent. And we don't stay with that, recognizing 'I am violent'; we invent non-violence. We say, 'I mustn't be violent'. Why bother with not being violent? You are violent. Let's see that, stay with that, hold with that, not move away from that, then we can examine it together and see how far we can go to dissipate it. But if you are constantly struggling to become non-violent you can't solve the problem, because when you are trying to become non-violent you are all the time sowing the seeds of violence. I am violent, I hope one day to be without violence, that one day is pretty far away, and during that interval I sow, I am still violent, perhaps not so much so but still violent. So, I say, don't let me bother with not being violent, let's understand violence, what is its nature, why it exists and is it possible to be free of it completely? That's much more interesting and vital than pursuing non-violence.

So similarly it is important to understand disorder, and forget about order. Because if we understand, and move out of that intellectual, verbal understanding, then we can find out how to live a life which is completely non-violent. I hope we are clear on this matter.

So, what is disorder? The brain is seeking order, it is not concentrated, attentive to discover what is disorder. This is a dialogue between you and the speaker. Don't wait for him to answer that question, then you will just repeat. If you can discover, find the truth of it, it is yours, then you can act, but if you merely listen to what the speaker is saying then you repeat, you don't know—'I don't understand, it is so difficult', and all the rest of that nonsense.

So what is disorder? To say one thing and think another, to act in one way, and hide your own thoughts, feelings, in another way. That is only a very simple matter. That requires great honesty, to say things that you mean—not what others have told you you mean. Probably all of you have read a great deal, so your brains are full of other people's knowledge, other people's concepts, prejudices, added to your own. So you repeat. You never sit down, or walk in the woods, and find out what is disorder. To find out, one has to have tremendous honesty—face things as they are. If I am afraid, I am afraid, I don't pretend I am not afraid. If I have told a lie, I say I have told a lie, not defend it. Face exactly what one is, not what one should be. Are we together in this? So gradually, or instantly, you find out for yourself the causation of any kind, either physical, or subjective, or psychological. Conflict exists when there are two opposing factors in life, the good and the bad. Is the good something totally separate from the bad? Or is the good partly bad? Am I making myself clear? No.

What is bad? And what is good? Obviously to kill another is bad, in the name of God, in the name of another human being, etc., etc. And what is good? To be good. Are you waiting for my description? Probably you have never gone into all this. Is the good separate from the bad? Or does the good have its roots, its beginning in the bad—you understand? There are two elements in human beings, the good and the bad. The bad, let's say, is to be angry, the good is not to be angry. But I have known anger and when I say, 'I mustn't be angry, I will be good,' the good is born out of my anger. When I say, 'I must be good' I have known the bad. If I don't know the bad I am the good. Not the goods! I am the good. I wonder if you understand this. That is, as long as I am violent I don't know what is the other. If I am not violent then the other is. So is the good born out of the bad? If it is born out of the bad, then the good is not good. Are we together in this? It seems rather mystifying, but please it is not. It is very simple. That is why I said, please let us think simply, clearly, without prejudice, without taking a bias.

So love is not hate—right? If love is born out of hate then it is not love. Is that clear? The speaker does not hate anybody, but suppose he does, then he says, 'I mustn't hate, I must love'—that is not love. It is still part of hate. It is a decision, it is an act of thought. And thought is not love.

So, can we, each one of us, feeling the responsibility that we have created this society in which we live, which is monstrous, immoral beyond imagination—can each one of us, living in this world, in this society, be utterly free from disorder? That means the complete end of conflict, the end of this feeling of duality in us—duality, the opposing elements in us. So is it not a matter of being tremendously aware—aware of every thought? Can we be that?

This leads up to a certain point: what is thought? What is thinking? If you are asked: what is thinking, what would be your answer? I am asking you, the speaker is asking you: what is thinking? And you begin to think. All our life is thinking and sensation. The child says, 'My book', 'That's my swing'—that is thinking. By thinking mankind has sent a rocket to the moon. But that thinking also put a flag up there. To go all that way to the moon and put up a flag! No, don't laugh. See what thought is doing.

Thought has created the whole world of technology. Astonishing things are being done of which we have very little imagination, which we know very little about—the computer, the extraordinary submarines and so on and so on. All that has been done by thinking—right? And thought has built the most extraordinary buildings. When you write a letter you have to think, when you drive a car you have to think, so thinking has become extraordinarily important for all of us. Thinking is part of our programme. We have been programmed: I am a Catholic, you are a Protestant, I am a Muslim, you are a Hindu, you are a Communist, I am a Democrat—you follow? It is part of our conditioning. We are being programmed by newspapers, magazines, the politicians, the priests, the archbishop, the Pope—you know the whole thing, how we are being programmed.

So thinking is what? Why do you think? Why do you think at all? Why don't you just act? You can't. First you design very carefully what you are going to do—is it right or wrong, is it as it should be or should not be?—and then your emotions, sensations say it is all right or all wrong, and you go and do it. All this is a process of thinking. Should I marry, should I not? That girl is right, that girl is not, or the other way round. Thinking has done an extraordinary amount of harm—war, hate, jealousy, wanting to hurt others. So what is thinking? The so-called good and the so-called bad thinking, right thinking and wrong thinking; it is still thinking. Oriental thinking and Western thinking; it is still thinking. What is thinking? Don't wait for me. Put to yourself that question. What is thinking? You cannot think without memory. Then what is memory? Go on. Put your brains into it. Remembrance, long association of ideas, long bundle of memories: I remember the house I lived in, I remember my childhood. That is what? The past. The past is memory. You don't know what will happen tomorrow but you can project what might happen. That is still the action of memory in time.

How does memory come? This is all so simple. Memory cannot exist without knowledge. If I have knowledge of my accident in a car which happened yesterday—it didn't—that accident is remembered. But previous to that remembrance there was the accident, which was the knowledge—right? The accident becomes knowledge, then from that knowledge comes memory. If I had had no accident there would be no memory of an accident. So knowledge is based on experience, and experience is always limited, always. I can't experience the immensity of order of the universe. I can't experience it, but I can imagine it. It is marvellous!

Experience is limited and therefore knowledge is limited, whether in the future or now because more and more knowledge is being added. Scientific knowledge is based on that. Knowledge is always limited whether now or in the future,

so memory is limited. So thought is limited. Right? This is where the difficulty is. Thought is limited. Whether it is noble or ignoble, religious, or non-religious, virtuous or not virtuous, moral or immoral, thought is still limited. Whatever thought does is limited. Are we together in this?

So, can thought bring about order because thought itself, being limited, may be the source of disorder? I wonder if you capture this? You understand my question? Very interesting. Go into it. Anything that is limited must create disorder; if I am a Muslim, which is very limited, I must create disorder; if I am an Israeli, I must create disorder, or a Hindu, a Buddhist, a Christian, and all the rest of it. So is thought the very root of disorder? Go into it, sir. Please be sceptical, don't accept a thing that the speaker says. Find out, investigate, not tomorrow, but now sitting there, go into it, find out. Put your passion into it, not your fanaticism. Then you will begin to discover.

So, as human beings, we have lived for millions of years in a state of violence, disorder, conflict—and all that is brought about by thought. All of it. So one begins to enquire: is there something else which is as active, as clear, as precise and energetic as thought? K discovered long ago that thought is very limited. Nobody told him; he discovered it, or came upon it. Then he began to ask, is there another instrument like that? Thought is within this brain, within this skull. The brain is the holder of all thought, all memories, all experience. It is also all emotion, sensation, nervous responses. It is the vast memory that is held there, racial, non-racial, personal —all that is there. And the centre of all that is thought. It may say, 'No, it is something else', but that is still thought. When it says it is seeking super-consciousness, it is still thought.

So one asks, K asks, is there another instrument, or not an instrument, a wave, a movement which is not of this kind? Are you asking this question? If you are asking it who is going to tell you? Be careful, please. This demands great subtlety, skill, because thought can be very deceptive. It says, 'All right I have understood, thought is limited', but it is still active. And then it begins to invent: 'I know thought is limited but God is limitless, and I am seeking God.' Thought is limited but it invents the rituals, the Middle Ages' robes of the monks and the priests and all the rest of it. So, can the brain *use* thought—act thoughtfully when it is necessary but otherwise, have no thought? You understand? Can the brain when necessary use thought? It is necessary to live with thought when you drive a car, when you eat, when you write a letter, when you do this or that. All that is the movement of limited thought—that is, when necessary, thought can act. But otherwise why should it chatter all day long?

So, is there another instrument which is not thought at all—which is not put together by thought, or conceived by thought, or manufactured subtly by thought? Find out. That requires the understanding of time. May I go into it? You aren't tired?

You have to understand what time is. Not the time of the rising and the setting of the sun, not the time of the new moon, not the time of day from morning until evening. Time is also all that happened in one's life, which are a thousand yesterdays, and all that might happen tomorrow. Time is horizontal and vertical. Time is the past, time is now, sitting here, and time is also tomorrow. And this is the cycle in which we are caught. A thousand yesterdays, many days in our life, and before we die there will be some more days. So this whole cyclical movement is time. Time is necessary to evolve from the little seed to the big tree, from the little baby to the grown-up man. There is physical time and also psychological time: I am this, but I will be that. To become *that* I need time. You are following all this? So, the brain lives in time. The brain has been cultivated, grown, evolved through time. This whole movement of life as we know it is time—right?

We know what was yesterday. You may remember your childhood, you may remember your life twenty years ago or ten days ago, which is the past. That past is the present, slightly changed, slightly modified by present circumstances. Are you following or am I talking to myself? Another ten minutes please. Don't go to sleep or get bored. It is your life we are talking about, not my life. It is your life, your daily life—what it actually is, not what it should be. Your daily, monotonous, lonely, desperate, anxious, uncertain life. And that life is part of the movement of time. Time is also the coming to an end when I die. So we are concerned with time. I will have a better job if I keep at it; if I get more skilful I will have more money. All that is time. And yesterday, many yesterdays, being slightly modified by circumstances, by pressure, is *now*. All that has happened from a thousand yesterdays becomes slightly polished, slightly modified and goes to the future—right? The past modifying itself through the present becomes the future. So the future is *now*. I wonder if you see this? Please give it just a little time.

One lived in India, with all the cultural, superstitious beliefs, dogmas, immense traditions, three to five thousand years old: one was brought up on that and one lived there in that little circle of Brahminism, and if one wasn't awake one remained there all the rest of one's life until one died. But circumstances, economic circumstances, travel, this and that, make one drop this;. the tradition of three to five thousand years is changed through modification, which is through economy: I have to earn more money; my wife, my children, must have more clothes. But the past is still moving and becomes changed through circumstances, and the change goes on into the future. That is clear. So you ask: what is the future? Is what you are now your future, modified, but still the future? There is a continuity from the past, slightly changing, to the future—right?

We have lived on this earth as human beings, homo sapiens, for millions of years. We were savages then and we still are savages, but with clean clothes, shaved, washed, polished, but inwardly we hate each other, we kill each other, we are tribalists, and all the rest of it. We haven't changed very much. So the future is *now*, because what I have been I still am, modified, and I will go on like that. So the future is *now*; and unless I break the cycle, the future will always be the now. I wonder if you understand this? It is not very difficult; please don't make it difficult. I have been greedy for the last thirty years and that greed becomes modified because I can't earn so much, satisfy myself, but I am still greedy; it goes on. So unless I stop greed *now*, tomorrow will be greedy. It is very simple.

So, our question then is: can 'what is', the past, change, end completely? Then you break the cycle. When you break the cycle the cells in the brain themselves change. We have discussed this matter with brain specialists—but don't bother with all that. You see, sir, I have lived ninety years—the speaker is ninety. Don't sympathize with me for God's sake. All that has happened during these ninety years, or fifty years, or ten years, or even ten days, is the past—memory, experiences, talking here, there, small audiences, big audiences, reputation and all that nonsense—and all that is in the past. And he feels important sitting on a platform, he has a reputation, and he must keep up that reputation. So he wants this reputation, this sitting on the platform, all that business, to continue—right? But he may get old—not may, he is old —and he may lose the audience because his brain might go gaga—no listen to it carefully, please listen; it is not a matter of laughter. It is funny, but just look at it. Unless he is free of the audience now, his reputation now—he will be stuck. So end it. He may go gaga next year, all right, but he has ended it. The brain has broken the cycle of time.

The brain is composed of millions and millions of cells and those very cells mutate. There is a different species of cell because you have moved away from a certain direction to another direction. You follow? That is, you have been going north all your life. Somebody comes along and says, 'Look, there is nothing in the north, for God's sake don't waste your energy on going north, go south or east.' The moment you turn east you have broken the pattern. You have broken the pattern which the brain cells have set and gone east. It is as simple as that, if one does it.

You can play with words endlessly, write books endlessly, but once you see the nature of time, you see that we have changed through these millions of years very little. We are still killing each other, only in a more diabolical way. The atom bomb can wipe us out in a second, vaporize us. We won't exist, nothing will exist. But it is the same when a man killed another man two million years ago. We are still doing that. Unless we break the pattern we will do that same thing tomorrow. This is very simple. They killed with a club two thousand years ago, later on they invented the arrow. The arrow, they thought, would stop all wars. Now we have the terrible means of destruction of the present day. It is the same as two million years ago; we are still killing. That is the pattern the brain has accepted, has lived with; the brain has created the pattern. If the brain can realize for itself, not through pressure, compulsion, but realize for itself that time has no value in the movement of change, then you have broken the pattern. Then there is a totally different way of living.

TALK THREE
SUNDAY, JULY 14

May we continue with our conversation?

We were talking about conflict and the causation of conflict. Conflict is growing more and more in the world, in every form, in every social section. We said that the cause of conflict is this constant opposition, not only within ourselves but also within the society in which we live. Society is what we have made it. I think that is fairly clear and obvious, because in ourselves we are, from the moment we are born till we die, in constant struggle, competition, conflict, with every form of destructive or positive attitudes, prejudices and opinions. This has been the way of our life, not only at the present period but also probably for the last two and a half million years. And we are still going on with this in the same pattern, the same mould—wars, more destructive than ever, division among nationalities, which is tribalism, religious divisions, family divisions, sectarian fragmentation and so on.

If we may point out again this morning we are not here as an intellectual group, or a rather romantic, imaginative, sentimental assembly. You and the speaker are going to take a journey together, not he leading you or you following him but together, side by side, perhaps holding hands if necessary.

We are taking a journey, rather complex, twisting, subtle and perhaps endless, a journey that has no beginning and no end. A journey as we understand it, has a beginning and an ending, something starts, goes on and then comes to an end, but perhaps it may not be at all like that. It may be a constant movement, not within the cycle of time but rather outside the field of momentum as we know it.

So we are *together*. Please, the speaker must insist on this point. You are not merely the listeners, accepting or rejecting what he says, but rather in co-operation, in responsibility, walking together in step, not one behind the other, along the same path, or lane. So it is your responsibility as well as the speaker's not to accept or to deny, to agree or disagree. We have been brought up, educated, in this system of agreeing and disagreeing. We agree with some things, we disagree entirely with other things, so there is always this division—those who agree, do something together, and those who are opposed to what they are doing.

Could we this morning banish from our brains altogether, entirely out of our blood, the idea of agreeing or disagreeing? Because if you agree with the speaker, and there are some who don't agree, then there is inevitably a conflict between the two. One may tolerate it, one may put up with it, accept it, but there is always this division—clear? So could we, seeing the consequences of agreeing and disagreeing, approving and disapproving, observe together, see together not only as far as we can what is happening externally—that is fairly simple because we are not told very much about what is actually going on in the political world, in the world of armaments, in the scientific world and all the technological worlds—but inwardly, subjectively, see exactly what is going on, not saying, 'Well, this is bad, this is good. I accept this, I don't accept that,' but just observe, not having in that observation any prejudice? Can we do that? Can we observe ourselves, our conduct, our behaviour, the way we think, our reactions, our faiths, beliefs, conclusions and so on? Could we observe all that as it is, not as it should be, or as it must be, but just look at it? That requires a great deal of attention, the brain must be extraordinarily active to reject any kind of reaction in watching oneself because, after all, what other people have said about us, the professors, the psychologists, the psychiatrists and the gurus is what *they* say; it is not what we see of ourselves. I hope we are following each other.

The words the speaker is using are very simple, words which we use daily in our conversation with each other. There is no jargon, no specialized linguistic, semantic jargon. We are talking things over together, as two friends using ordinary, daily language. So we are asking: can we see exactly what we are without taking sides about it, not agreeing and disagreeing, seeing the consequences of each attitude, assessing, evaluating, judging, but just observing as you observe the sky of an evening full of stars, and those mountains, majestic against the blue sky? Can we in the same way observe ourselves and our relationship to the world, and the world's relationship to us? It is a rather complex process. Are we together? Or am I marching ahead and leaving you behind? Could we go together, keeping in step?

What are we? Why have we such deep-rooted self-interest? Not only self-interest outwardly—outwardly there is a certain necessity for self-interest otherwise one has to give up—but inwardly, psychologically, subjectively? Why is there such deep, impenetrable self-interest in all of us? Self-interest—you know what that word means? To be interested in oneself, one's own profits, one's own failures, one's own fragmentation, one's own prejudices, opinions, the whole content of one's life. Self-interest—why is it that we are so committed to that? Is it possible to live in this world without that self-interest—first psychologically and then seeing if it is possible externally? Are we together or am I talking over beyond that tent, over the fence?

Have you ever noticed that we build a fence round ourselves: a fence of self-protection, a fence to ward off any hurts, a barrier between you and the other, between you and the family, and so on? There is a barrier between you and the speaker. Naturally. You don't know the speaker, the speaker doesn't know you, therefore you are rather politely listening, curious as to what the devil he is talking about and hoping you will get something out of it after sitting an hour or so in this hot tent, expecting something, curious, choosing what suits you, what doesn't suit you, listening partially, not entirely because one doesn't want to expose oneself to oneself, so naturally one creates either a very, very thin barrier, hardly any, or a definite wall. Why do we do that? Is that not also self-interest? And this self-interest must inevitably bring about fragmentation, to break up. Nationally, you can see the barrier—on one side England and the other side all

Europe, and beyond it. There is this constant division, and where there is division there must be conflict, that is inevitable. Whether you have a very deep intimate relationship with your wife or husband, a girl or boy, and so on, where there is division there must be fragmentation, there must be conflict. That is a law—right? Whether you like it or not that is a law. But when one sees that, then the very seeing is the way of breaking down the barrier.

So we must enquire: what does it mean to see? What does it mean to observe? I am observing myself—right? I am watching what I am, my recreations, my prejudices, my convictions, my idiosyncrasies, the traditions in which I have been brought up, the reputation, all that rubbish. I am watching. If I do not watch very, very carefully, listen to every sound that is going on in watching, then I set a direction in which I must go. You are following all this? Am I talking to myself?

We were talking in Washington, America, and they clapped what I said, approving, encouraging. Here, you all sit very quietly. One doesn't know whether you are really walking together with the speaker, actually listening, or casually coming to a Sunday morning sermon. Instead of going to church you turn up here, either for amusement, or just to hear what that chap is saying, or, 'Well I agree with him in some things but he is not quite right about other things.' We never look at the whole thing, the whole problem of life, the whole of existence from childhood to death. We never take the whole thing in and observe, learn, not accumulate knowledge, that is fairly simple, but learn what is happening in ourselves, the demands that we make upon each other, the hurts, the deep loneliness, the depression, the anxiety, the uncertainty, the fears, and all the pleasant things that we have, and also the suffering, and ultimately the pain of death. We never look at this whole movement as one, but rather we consider it fragmentarily.

Now we are going to look together if we may, not only at what is the cause of this fragmentation but also whether the brain, which has been conditioned for millions of years to war, to conflict, to work, work, work all the time, endlessly chattering, divided as nationalities and so on—your god and my god, Eastern philosophy opposed to Western philosophy—whether the brain can put aside altogether the whole movement of agreeing and disagreeing, in which there is choice. I choose to go this way and you choose to go that way; I choose to believe in God, or no god, and you say, 'No, sorry, I can't accept that, there must be God, because I believe it, I like it'—or 'It is my tradition'—and so on. If we once recognize the division, the agreement, the disagreement, reward and punishment, then we can begin to look actually at ourselves, because ourselves is the world. What we are, the world is. If we are violent, suspicious, ungenerous, the world is like that. This is obvious because we have made this society, this monstrous, ugly, immoral world in which we live, with all the gods. It has become a great circus, a painful circus, or a pleasurable circus. So can we see exactly what we are without any distortion? What are we—psychologically, not biologically? Biologically we have been put together through millennia upon millennia. Psychologically, from the beginning of man, there has been violence, hate, jealousy, aggression, trying always to become something more, more, more, and much more than what we are. Is it that we are listening merely to the description or do we see the fact, not the idea of the fact? You understand? There is a difference between fact and the idea of the fact. That is, we have an idea, see something and then pursue the idea: 'I shouldn't be like this, I must be like that.' That is an idea. When I see exactly what I am, that is a fact. Fact does not need an idea, a concept, an ideology. It is so. I am angry. That is a fact. But if I say, 'I must not be angry', then it becomes an idea. Are we together in this?

So what is it you are making out of this? Is it that you are concluding a set of ideas, or are you seeing the fact as it is—that we are jealous, aggressive, lonely, fearful and all the rest of it? The whole psyche, the persona, the ego, is all that, and all that is the past, the memories we have collected—right? I have been afraid, I know what fear is, and the moment that feeling arises I say, 'That is fear.' That very saying 'That it is fear' is an idea, not a fact. I don't know if you are following all this? Sir, the word tree is not the actual tree. The name K is not the actual K. The word is not the thing. So, when you observe, your brain is caught in a whole network of words, words, words. Can you look at yourself without the word? Oh, come on, sirs, play the game with me, will you? The ball is in your court. That is, can you look at your wife, at your husband, at your children, or your girl friend, or whatever it is, without the word? Without the image? That word, that image, is the division. Can you look at the speaker without the word?—the word being all the remembrances about the speaker, the reputation, what you have read or not read, and so on, but just observe. Which means one must grasp, understand, how the brain operates—your own brain, not the brain of philosophers, or the spiritual writers, or the priests or somebody or other. Just observe yourself without the word, then you can look at certain facts, why human beings get hurt. That is very important to find out.

From childhood we are hurt. There is always the pressure, always the sense of being rewarded and punished. You say something to me which I get angry about and that hurts me—right? So we have realized a very simple fact that from childhood we are hurt, and for the rest of our life we carry that hurt—afraid of being hurt further, or attempting not to be hurt, which is another form of resistance. So, are we aware of these hurts and of therefore creating a barrier round ourselves, the barrier of fear? Can we go into this question of fear? Shall we? Not for my pleasure, for it is you I am talking about. Can we go into it very, very deeply and see why human beings, which is all of us, have put up with fear for thousands of years? We see the consequences of fear—fear of not being rewarded, fear of being a failure, fear of your weakness, fear of your own feeling that you must come to a certain point and not being able to. Are you interested in going into this problem? It means going into it completely to the very end, not just saying, 'Sorry, that is too difficult.' Nothing is too difficult if you want to do it. The word difficult prevents you from further action. But if you can put away that word difficult then we can go into this very, very complex problem.

First, why do we put up with it? If you have a car which goes wrong you go to the nearest garage, if you can, and then the machinery is put right and you go on. Is it that there is no one we can go to who will help us to have no fear—you understand the question? Do we want help from somebody to be free of fear—from psychologists, psycho-therapists, psychiatrists, or the priest, or the guru who says, 'Surrender everything to me, including your money, then you will be perfectly all right'? We do this. You may laugh, you may be amused, but we are doing this all the time inwardly.

So, do we want help? Prayer is a form of help; asking to be free from fear is a form of help. The speaker telling you how to be free of fear is a form of help. But he is not going to tell you how, because we are walking together, we are giving energy to discover for ourselves the causation of fear. If you see something very clearly, then you don't have to decide, or choose, or ask for help—you act—right? Do we see clearly the whole structure, the inward nature of fear? You have been afraid and the memory of it comes back and says that is fear. You understand what I am saying?

So let's go into this carefully—not the speaker going into it and then you agreeing, or disagreeing, but you yourself taking the journey with the speaker, not verbally or intellectually, but delving, probing, investigating. We are finding out; we want to delve as you dig in the garden or to find water. You dig deep, you don't stand outside on the earth and say,

'I must have water.' You dig or go to the river. So first of all, let's be very clear: do you want help in order to be free of fear? If you want help then you are responsible for establishing an authority, a leader, a priest. So one must ask oneself before we go into this question of fear, whether you want help. Of course you go to a doctor if you have pain, or a headache, or some kind of disease. He knows much more about your organic nature so he tells you what to do. We are not talking about that kind of help. We are talking about whether you need help, somebody to instruct you, to lead you, and to say, 'Do this, do that, day after day and you will be free of fear.' The speaker is not helping you. That is one thing certain, because you have dozens of helpers, from the great religious leaders—God forbid!—to the lowest, the poor psychologist round the corner. So let us be very clear between ourselves that the speaker doesn't want to help you in *any* way psychologically. Would you kindly accept that? Honestly accept it? Don't say yes, it is very difficult. In all your life you have sought help in various directions, though some say, 'No, I don't want help.' It requires not only outward perception to see what the demand for help has done to humanity. You ask help only when you are confused, when you don't know what to do, when you are uncertain. But when you see things clearly—see, observe, perceive, not only externally, but much more inwardly—when you see things very, very clearly you don't want any help; there it is. And from that comes action. Are we together in this? Let's repeat this if you don't mind. The speaker is not telling you *how*. Never ask that question *how*, for then there is always somebody giving you a rope. The speaker is not helping you in *any* way, but together we are walking along the same road, perhaps not at the same speed. Set your own speed and we will walk together. Clear? We are in accord?

If you are not clear about demanding help you will have to go somewhere else. Probably you will. Or turn to a book, or turn to somebody, not towards the speaker. Sorry to depress you and say I won't stretch out my hand; that is not it. If we are walking together we are holding hands. There is no stretching out your hand and seeking help. Are we working together? Or am I working and getting hot about it?

What is the cause of fear? Go slowly please. Cause. If you can discover the cause then you can do something about it, you can change the cause—right? If a doctor tells me, tells the speaker, he has got cancer—which he hasn't—but suppose he tells me that I have got cancer and says, 'I can remove it easily and you will be all right', I go to him. He removes it and the cause comes to an end. So the cause can always be changed, rooted out. If you have got a headache you can find the cause of it; you may be eating wrongly, or smoking or drinking too much. Either you stop your drinking, smoking and all the rest, or you take a pill to stop it. The pill then becomes the effect which stops for the moment the causation —right? So cause and effect can always be changed, immediately or you take time over it. If you take time over it, then during that interval other factors enter into it. So you never change the effect, you continue with the cause. Are we together in this? So what is the cause of fear? Why haven't we gone into it? Why do we tolerate it, knowing the effect of fear, the consequences of fear? If you are not at all afraid psychologically, have no fear at all, you would have no gods, you would have no symbols to worship, no personalities to adore. Then you are psychologically extraordinarily free. Fear also makes one shrink, apprehensive, wanting to escape from it and therefore the escape becomes more important than the fear. Are you following? So we are going to go over it together to find out what is the cause of fear—the root cause of it. And if we discover it for ourselves, then it is over. If you see the causation, or many causes, then that very perception ends the cause. Are you listening to me, the speaker, to explain the causation? Or have you never even asked such a question? I have borne fear, as has my father, my grandfather, the whole race in which I am born, the whole community; the whole structure of gods and rituals is based on fear and the desire to achieve some extraordinary state.

So, let us go into this. We are not talking about the various forms of fear—fear of darkness, fear of one's husband, wife, fear of society, fear of dying, etc. It is like a tree that has got many, many branches, many flowers, many fruits, but we are talking about the very root of that tree. The root of it—not your particular form of fear. You can trace your particular form to the very root. So we are asking: are we concerned with *our* fears, or with the *whole fear*? With the whole tree, not just one branch of it? Because unless you understand how the tree lives, the water it requires, the depth of the soil and so on, merely trimming the branches won't do anything; we must go to the very root of fear.

So what is the root of fear? Don't wait for me to answer. I am *not* your leader, I am *not* your helper, I am *not* your guru—thank God! We are together, as two brothers, and I mean it, the speaker *means* it, it is not just words. As two good friends who have known each other from the beginning of time, walking along the same path, at the same speed, looking at everything that is around you and in you, so together we will go into it. Please, together. Otherwise it becomes just words, and at the end of the talk you will say, 'Really what am I to do with my fear?'

Fear is very complex. It is a tremendous reaction. If you are aware of it, it is a shock, not only biologically, organically, but also a shock to the brain. The brain has a capacity, as one discovers, not from what others say, to remain healthy in spite of a shock. I don't know all about it, but the very shock invites its own protection. If you go into it yourself, you will see. So fear is a shock—momentarily, or continuing in different forms, with different expressions, in different ways. So we are going to the very, very, very root of it. To understand the very root of it, we must understand time—right? Time as yesterday, time as today, time as tomorrow. I remember something I have done, of which I am shy, or nervous, or apprehensive, or fearful; I remember all that and it continues to the future. I have been angry, jealous, envious—that is the past. I am still envious, slightly modified; I am fairly generous about things but envy goes on. This whole process is time, isn't it? You understand? Say yes, for God's sake! No, don't say yes!

Let's begin again. What do you consider is time? By the

clock, sunrise, sunset, the evening star, the new moon with the full moon coming a fortnight later? What is time to you? Time to learn a skill? Time to learn a language? Time to write a letter? Time to go to your house from here? All that is time as distance—right? I have to go from here to there. That is a distance covered by time. But time is also inward, psychological: I am this, I must become that. Becoming that is called evolution. Evolution means from the seed to the tree. And also I am ignorant but I will learn. I don't know, but I will know. Give me time to be free of violence. You are following all this? Give me time. Give me a few days, a month, or a year and I will be free of it. So we live by time—not only going to the office every day from nine to five, God forbid, but also time to become something. Look, you understand all this? Right? Time, the movement of time? I have been afraid of you and I remember that fear; that fear is still there and I will be afraid of you tomorrow. I hope not, but if I don't do something very drastic about it I will be afraid of you tomorrow. So we live by time. Please, let's be clear about this. We live by time, which is, I am living, I will die. I will postpone death as long as possible; I am living and I am going to do everything to avoid death though it is inevitable. So psychologically as well as biologically we live by time.

Is time a factor of fear? Please enquire. Time—that is, I have told a lie, I don't want you to know, but you are very smart; you look at me and say, 'You have told a lie.' 'No, no, I have not'—I protect myself instantly because I am afraid of your finding out that I am a liar. I am afraid because of something I have done, which I don't like you to know. Which is what? Thought, isn't it? I have done something which I remember, and that remembrance says, be careful, don't let him discover that you told a lie because you have got a good reputation as an honest man, so protect yourself. So, thinking and time are together. There is no division between thought and time. Please be clear on this matter, otherwise you will get rather confused later. The causation of fear is time/thought, the root of it—right?

Are we clear on this thing that time, that is, the past, with all the things that one has done, and thought, whether pleasant or unpleasant, specially if it is unpleasant, is the root of fear? This is an obvious fact. A very simple verbal fact. But to go behind the word and see the truth of this time/thought, you will inevitably ask: how is thought to stop? It is a natural question, no? If thought creates fear, which is so obvious, then how am I to stop thinking? 'Please help me to stop my thinking.' I would be an ass to ask such a question but I am asking it. How am I to stop thinking? Is that possible? Go on, sir, investigate, don't let me go on. Thinking. We live by thinking. Everything we do is through thought. We went into that carefully the other day. We won't waste time going into the cause, the beginning of thinking, how it comes—experience, knowledge, which is always limited, memory and then thought. I am just briefly repeating it.

So, is it possible to stop thinking? Is it possible not to chatter all day long, to give the brain a rest, though it has its own rhythm, the blood going up to it, its own activity? Its own, not the activity imposed by thought—you understand?

May I point out, may the speaker point out, that that is a wrong question. Who is it that stops thinking? It is still thought, isn't it? When I say, 'If I could only stop thinking then I would have no fear', who is it that wishes to stop thought? It is still thought, isn't it, because it wants something else?

So, what will you do? Any movement of thought to be other than what it is, is still thinking. I am greedy, but I must not be greedy—it is still thinking. Thinking has put together all the paraphernalia, all that business that goes on in churches. Like this tent it has been carefully put together by thought. Apparently thought is the very root of our existence. So we are asking a very serious question, seeing what thought has done, invented the most extraordinary things, the computer, the warships, the missiles, the atom bomb, surgery, medicine, and also the things it has made man do, go to the moon and so on. Thought is the very root of fear. Do we see that? Not how to end thought, but see actually that thinking is the root of fear, which is time? Seeing, not the words, but actually seeing. When you have severe pain, the pain is not different from you and you act instantly—right? So do you see as clearly as you see the clock, the speaker and your friend sitting beside you, that thought is the causation of fear? Please don't ask: 'How am I to see?' The moment you ask how, someone is willing to help you, then you become their slave. But if you yourself see that thought/time are really the root of fear, it doesn't need deliberation or a decision. A scorpion is poisonous, a snake is poisonous—at the very perception of them you act.

So one asks, why don't we *see*? Why don't we see that one of the causes of war is nationalities? Why don't we see that one may be called a Muslim, and another a Christian—why do we fight over names, over propaganda? Do we see it, or just memorize or think about it? You understand, sirs, that your consciousness is the rest of mankind. Mankind, like you and others, goes through every form of difficulty, pain, travail, anxiety, loneliness, depression, sorrow, pleasure—every human being goes through this—*every* human being all over the world. So our consciousness, our being, is the entire humanity. This is so. How unwilling we are to accept such a simple fact, because we are so accustomed to individuality—I, me, first. But if you see that your consciousness is shared by *all* other human beings living on this marvellous earth then your whole way of living changes. But you don't see that. You need argument, you need lots of persuasion, pressure, propaganda, which are all so terribly useless because it is you that has to see this thing for yourself.

So, can we, each of us, who are the rest of mankind, who are mankind, look at a very simple fact? Observe, see, that the causation of fear is thought/time? Then the very perception is action. And from that you don't rely on *anybody*. The guru is like you. The leader may put on different robes and all the jewels, but strip him of all that and he is just like you and me, only he has achieved greater power, and we also want greater power, money, position, status. So could we look at all this, see it very clearly; then that very perception ends all this rubbish. Then you are a free person.

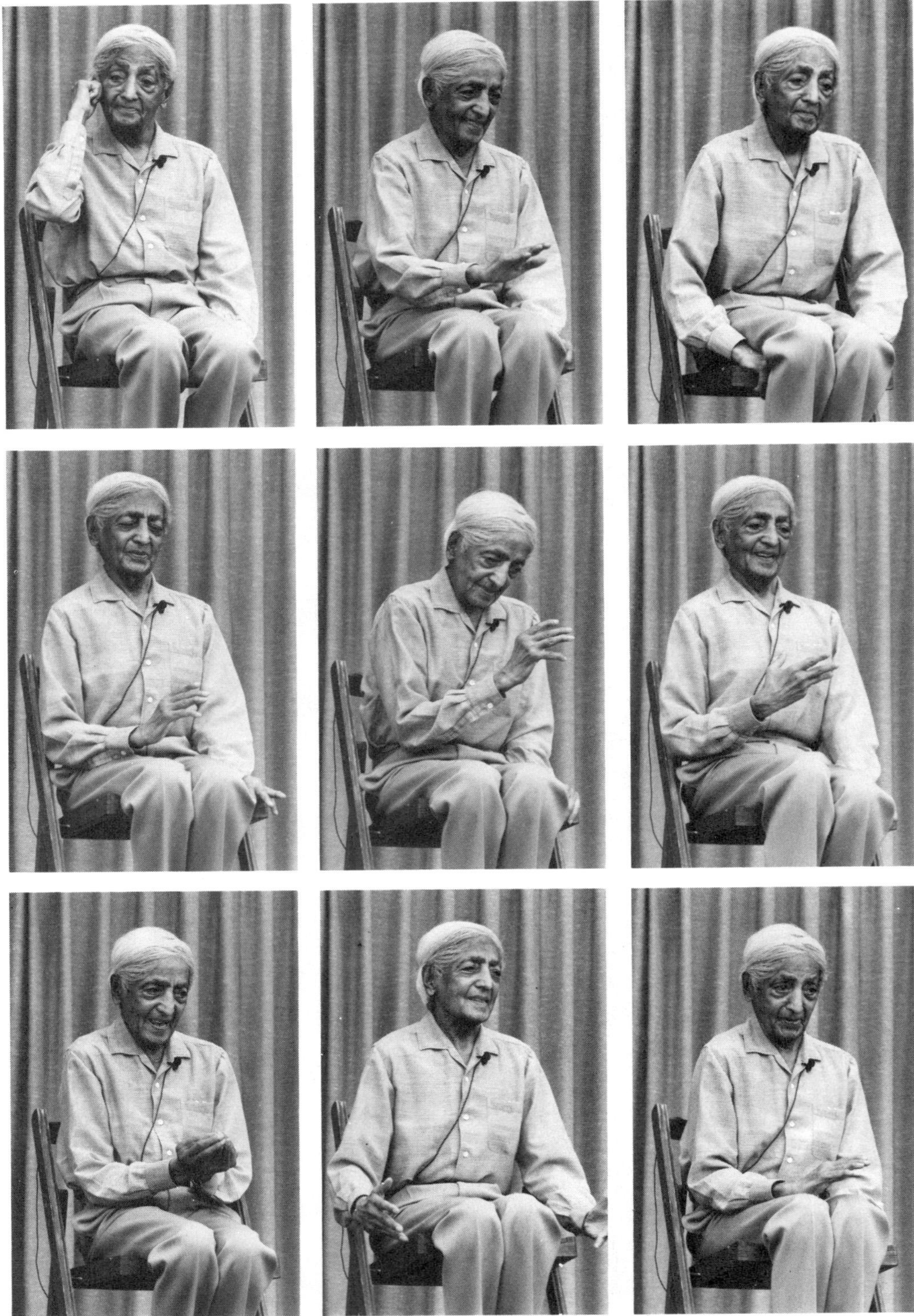

TALK FOUR
WEDNESDAY, JULY 17

You heard all the announcements. May I also announce that I am going to talk? And also that you are going to share in the talk. It is not a solo, but together, and the speaker means together, not that he is leading you or helping you or trying to persuade you, but rather together, and that word is important—together we take a very, very long journey. It is rather a difficult path—I won't use that word, that is a dangerous word—a lane, a way that will be rather complex because we are going to talk about self-interest, austerity, conduct and whether it is possible in our daily life to end all sorrow. This is a very important question: why humanity after so many thousands and thousands of years has never been free from sorrow, not only each one's sorrow, the pain, the anxiety, the loneliness involved in that sorrow, but also the sorrow of mankind. We are going to talk about that. And also, if we have time, we are going to talk about pleasure, and also *death*.

It is such a lovely morning, beautiful, clear blue sky, the quiet hills and the deep shadows, and the running waters, the meadow, the grove and the green grass, so should we talk over together what beauty is on such a lovely morning because that is also a very important question? Not the beauty of nature or the extraordinary vitality, dynamic energy of a tiger. You have probably only seen tigers in a zoo where the poor things are kept for your amusement. In some parts of the world where the speaker has been, he was close to a wild tiger, as close as two feet.

We should go into this question because without beauty and love there is no truth. We ought to examine very closely the word beauty. What is beauty? You are asking that question and so is the speaker; we are both looking together, not only at the word, but at the implications of that word, at the immensity, the incalculable depth of beauty. We can talk about it, but the talk, the words, the explanations and the descriptions are not beauty. The word beauty is not beauty. Beauty is something totally different. So one must be, if one may point out, very alert to words because our brain works, is active, in a movement of words. Words convey what one feels, what one thinks, and the brain accepts explanations and descriptions because most of our brain structure is verbal. So one must go into it very, very carefully, not only with regard to beauty but also with regard to austerity and self-interest. We shall go into all these questions this morning, if we will.

So we are asking ourselves: What is beauty? Is beauty in a person, in a face? Is beauty in museums, in painting—classical paintings, modern paintings? Is beauty in music—Beethoven, Mozart, Bach and all the noise that is going on in the world called music? Is beauty in a poem? In literature? Dancing? Is all that beauty? Or is beauty something entirely different? We are going into it together. Please, if one may respectfully point out, don't accept the words, don't merely be satisfied with the description and explanations, but let us, if we can, put from our brain all agreeing and disagreeing and look at it very carefully, stay with it, penetrate into the word.

As we said, without that quality of beauty, which is sensitivity, there is no truth. That quality implies not only the beauty of nature—the deserts, the forests, the rivers and the vast mountains with their immense dignity, majesty, but also the feeling of it, not romantic imaginings and sentimental states—those are merely sensations. Is beauty, then, we are asking, a sensation? Because we live by sensations—sexual sensation, with which goes pleasure, and also the pain involved in the feeling that it is not being fulfilled, and so on. So could we this morning put out of our brain all those words and go into this enormous, very complicated, subtle question: what is the nature of beauty? We are not writing a poem.

When you look at those mountains, those immense rocks jutting into the sky—if you look at them quietly you feel the immensity of it, the enormous majesty of it, and for the moment, for the second, the tremendous dignity of it, the solidity of it, puts away all your thoughts, your problems—right? And you say, 'How marvellous that is.' So what has taken place there? The majesty of those mountains, the very immensity of the sky and the blue and the snow-clad mountains, drives away for a second all your problems. It makes you totally forget yourself for a second. You are enthralled by it, you are struck by it, like a child, who has been naughty all day long, or naughty for a while, which he has a right to be, and is given a complicated toy. He is absorbed by the toy until he breaks it. The toy has taken him over and he is quiet, he is enjoying it. He has forgotten his family, the 'Do this, don't do that': the toy becomes the most exciting thing for him.

In the same way, the mountains, the river, the meadows and the groves absorb you, you forget yourself. Is that beauty? To be absorbed by the mountains, by the river, or the green fields, means that you are like a child absorbed by a toy, and for the moment you are quiet, taken over, surrendering yourself to something. Is that beauty? Being taken over? You understand? Surrendering yourself to something great and that thing forcing you for a second to forget yourself? Then you depend, depend as the child does on a toy, or on the cinema or television, when for the moment you have identified yourself with the actor or actress. Would you consider that state—being taken over, surrendering, being absorbed—would you consider that that quiet second is beauty? When you go to a church or a temple or a mosque, the chanting, the rituals, the intonation of the voice, are carefully organized to create a certain sensation, which you call worship, which you call a sense of religiosity. Is that beauty? Or is beauty something entirely different? Are we understanding this question together?

Is there beauty where there is self-conscious endeavour? Or is there beauty only when the self is not—when the me, the observer, is not? So is it possible without being absorbed, taken over, surrendering, to be in that state without the self, without the ego, without the me always thinking about itself? Is that at all possible, living in this modern world with all its

specializations, its vulgarity, its immense noise—not the noise of running waters, of the song of a bird? Is it possible to live in this world without the self, the me, the ego, the persona, the assertion of the individual? In that state, when there is really freedom from all this, only then is there beauty. You may say, 'That is too difficult, that is not possible.'

But I am asking: is it possible to live in this world without self-interest? What does self-interest mean? What are the implications of that word? How far can we be without self-interest and live here, in the bustle, the noise, the vulgarity, the competition, the personal ambitions, and so on and so on? We are going together to find out.

Self-interest hides in many ways, hides under every stone and every act—hides in prayer, in worship, in having a successful profession, great knowledge, a special reputation, like the speaker. When there is a guru who says, 'I know all about it. I will tell you all about it'—is there not self-interest there? This seed of self-interest has been with us for a million years. Our brain is conditioned to self-interest. If one is aware of that, just aware of it, not saying, 'I am not self-interested or how can one live without self-interest?' but just be aware, then how far can one go, how far can one investigate into oneself to find out for ourselves, each one of us, how in action, in daily activity, in our behaviour, how deeply one can live without a sense of self-interest?

So, if we will, we will examine all that. Self-interest divides, self-interest is the greatest corruption (the word corruption means to break things apart) and where there is self-interest there is fragmentation—your interest as opposed to my interest, my desire opposed to your desire, my urgency to climb the ladder of success opposed to yours. Just observe this; you can't do anything about it—you understand?—but just observe it, stay with it and see what is taking place. If you have ever dismantled a car, as the speaker has done, you know all the parts, you learn all about it, you know how it works. (I am talking of the 1925 cars; at that period they were very simple, very direct, very honest, strong, beautiful cars.) And when you know about it mechanically, you can feel at ease; you know how fast to go, how slow, etc. So if we are aware of our own self-interest, we begin to learn about it—right? You don't say, 'I must be against it, or for it, or how can I live without it or who are you to tell me about myself?'

When you begin to be aware choicelessly of your self-interest, to stay with it, to study it, to learn about it, to observe all the intricacies of it, then you can find out for yourself where it is necessary and where it is completely unnecessary. It is necessary for daily living—to have food, clothes and shelter and all the physical things—but psychologically, inwardly, is it necessary to have any kind of self-interest? For that let us investigate relationship. In our relationship with each other there is mutual self-interest. You satisfy me and I satisfy you; you use me and I use you. Where there is self-interest there must be fragmentation, breaking up—right? I am different from you—self-interest.

What is relationship? Relationship to the earth, to all the beauty of the world, to nature and to other human beings and to one's wife, husband, girl friend, boy friend and so on:

what is that bondage, what is that thing about which we say, 'I am related'? Please investigate this together. Don't, please, rely on the description the speaker is indulging in. Let's look at it closely.

What is relationship? When there is no relationship we feel so lonely, depressed, anxious—you know, the whole series of movements hidden in the structure of self-interest. What is relationship? When you say, 'My wife', 'My husband', what does it mean? When you are related to God, if there is a God, what does it mean? That word relationship is very important to understand. I am related to my wife, to my children, to my family. Let's begin there. That is the core of all society, the family. In the Asiatic world especially, family means a great deal; it is tremendously important to them—the son, the nephew, the grandmother, grandfather. It is the centre on which all society is based. So when one says, 'My wife', 'my girl', 'my friend', what does that mean? Most of you are probably married, or have a girl friend or a boy friend. What does it mean to be related to them? What are you related to?

Let's move away for a moment from the wife and husband. When you follow somebody, a guru, a prophet, a politician, the speaker, or some other person, what is it you are following, what is it that you are surrendering, giving up? Is it the image that you have created about the speaker or the guru, or the image you have in your brain that it is the right thing to do and therefore you will follow him? Is it the image, the picture, the symbol, that you have built and that you are following, not the person, not what he is saying? The speaker has been talking for the last seventy years. I am sorry for him! And unfortunately he has established some reputation, with the books and all that business, so you have naturally created an image about him and you are following that; not what the teaching says. The teaching says, 'Don't follow anybody.' But you have built the image, and you are following that which you desire, which satisfies you, which is of tremendous self-interest—right?

Now let's come back to the wife and husband. When you say, 'My wife', what do you mean by that word, what is the content of that word, what is behind the word? Look at it. Is it all the memories, the sensations, pleasure, pain, anxiety, jealousy—is all that embodied in the word wife or husband? The husband is ambitious, wants to achieve a better position, more money, and the wife not only remains at home but has her own ambitions, her own desires. So there they are. They may get into bed together, but the two are separate all the time. Let's be simple with these facts, and honest. There is always conflict. One may not be aware of it and say, 'Oh, no, we have no conflict between us', but scrape that a little bit with a heavy shovel, or with a scalpel, and you will find that the root of all this is self-interest. And there may be self-interest in the professionals. Of course there is—doctors, scientists, philosophers, priests, the whole thing is desire for fulfilment. We are not exaggerating, we are simply stating 'what is', not trying to cover it up, not trying to get beyond it: there it is. That is the seed in which we are born, and that seed goes on flowering, growing till we die. And when we try to control self-interest, that very control is another form of self-interest. How cleverly self-interest operates. And it also hides behind austerity.

So now we have to examine what we mean by austerity. What is austerity? The whole world, especially the religious world, has used that word, has laid down certain laws about it, specially for the monks in various monasteries. (In India there are no monasteries except for Buddhists. There are no organized monasteries, fortunately.) So what do we mean by that word austere with which goes great dignity? We looked up that word in the dictionary. It comes from Greek, to have a dry mouth, that is, dry, harsh, not just the mouth. Harsh. Is that austere? Harsh: to deny oneself the luxury of a hot bath, to have few clothes, or to wear a particular form of robe, or take a vow to be celibate, to be poor or to fast or sit up straight endlessly, to control all one's desires. Surely all that is not austerity. It is all outward show.

So is there an austerity that is not a sensation, that is not contrived, that is not cajoled, that does not say, 'I will be austere in order to . . .'? Is there an austerity that is not visible at all to another? You are understanding all this? Is there an austerity that has no discipline—that has a sense of a wholeness inwardly in which there is no craving, no breaking up, no fragmentation? With that austerity goes dignity, quietness.

One has also to understand the nature of desire. That may be the root of the whole structure of self-interest. Desire. Are we together in this? Desire is a great sensation—right? Desire is the senses coming into activity. As we said earlier, sensation is of great importance to us—sensation of sex, sensation of new experience, sensation of meeting somebody

who is well known. (I must tell you this lovely story. A friend of ours met the Queen of England and shook hands with her. After it was over a person came up to her and said, 'May I shake hands with you because you have shaken hands with the Queen?'!)

We live always by sensation—sensation of being secure—please watch it—sensation of having fulfilled, sensation of great pleasure, gratification and so on. What relationship has sensation to desire? Is desire something separate from sensation? Go into this, please. It is important to understand this thing. I am not explaining it. We are looking at it together. What is the relationship of desire to sensation? When does sensation become desire? Or are they inseparable? You follow? Do they always go together—right? Are you working as hard as the speaker is working? Or are you just saying, 'Yes, go on with it'? Or have you heard this before and say, 'Oh God, he has gone back to that again'?

You know that the more you understand the activity of thought, the deeper you get to the root of thought; then you begin to understand so many things. Then you see the whole phenomenon of the world, nature, the truth of nature; then you ask, 'What is truth?' I won't go into all that for the moment.

Our life is based on sensation and desire, and we are asking: what is the actual relationship between the two? When does sensation become desire? You are following this? At what second does desire become dominant? I see a beautiful camera, with all the latest improvements. I lift it and look at it, and there is sensation of observation—seeing the beautifully made, very complex camera of great value as a pleasure of possession, a pleasure of taking photos. Then what is that sensation to do with desire? When does that desire begin to flower into action, and say, 'I must have it'?

Have you observed the movement of sensation, whether it is sexual, whether it is walking in the valleys or climbing the hills, overlooking all the world from a great height, or seeing a lovely garden when you have only a little lawn around your place? You see this; then what takes place that turns the sensation into desire? You are following all this? Please don't go to sleep. It is too lovely a morning. Stay with this question: what is the relationship of sensation to desire? Stay with it, do not try and find an answer, but look at it, observe it, see the implications of it; then you will discover that sensation, which is natural, is transformed into desire when thought creates the image out of that sensation. That is, there is a sensation of seeing that very expensive, beautiful camera; then thought comes along and says, 'I wish I had that camera.' So thought creates the image out of that sensation and at that moment desire is born. Look at it yourself, go into it. You don't need any book, any philosopher, anybody—just look at it, patiently, tentatively, then you will come upon it very quickly. That is, sensation is a slave to thought, and thought creates an image, and at that moment desire is born. And we live by desire: 'I must have this.' 'I don't want it.' 'I must become . . .' You follow? This whole movement of desire.

Now what relationship has desire to self-interest? We are pursuing the same thread. As long as there is desire, which is creating the image out of sensation by thought, there must be self-interest. Whether I want to reach heaven, or become a bank manager, or a rich person, it is the same. Whether you want to achieve heaven or become rich it is exactly the same. If one person desires to be a saint and another to have some great skill it is exactly the same thing. One is called religious, the other is called worldly. How words cripple us.

So we must come to the question: what is sorrow? Is it that sorrow exists as long as there is self-interest? Please go into it. If you understand all this you don't have to read a single book. If you really live with this thing, the gates of heaven are open—not heaven, you understand, that is just a form of speech. So I am asking a very serious question which has haunted man from the beginning of his existence: what is sorrow, the tears, the laughter, the pain, the anxiety, the loneliness, the despair? And can it ever end? Or is man doomed for ever to live with sorrow? Everyone on the earth, *everyone*, whether they are highly placed or nobody at all, *everyone* goes through this turmoil of sorrow, the shock of it, the pain of it, the uncertainty of it, the utter loneliness of it. The sorrow of a poor man who doesn't know how to read or write, has but one meal a day and sleeps on the pavement is like you; he has his own sorrow. There is the sorrow of millions of people who have been slaughtered by the powerful, by the bigoted, tortured by religions—the infidel and the believer—you understand all this? Christianity especially has murdered more people than anything else—sorry!

So there is sorrow. What does that word mean? Is it a mere

remembrance of something you have lost? You had a brother, son or wife, who died, and you have the picture, the photo of them on the piano, or mantelpiece, or next to your bed, and you have the memories of all those days when they were alive. Is that sorrow? Is sorrow engendered, cultivated by memory? You understand my question? When someone is cut down by death, by accident, old age, or whatever it is, and the memory continues, is that sorrow? Is sorrow related to memory? Come on, sirs.

I had a son, or a brother, or a mother I liked—I will use the word like for the moment. I call that 'like' love. I liked those people very much. I lived with them. I have chatted with them. We played together. All that memory is stored. And my son, my brother, my mother, or somebody, dies, is taken away, gone forever, and I feel a shock, I feel terribly lonely and shed tears. And I run off to church, temple, pick up a book, do this or that, to escape; or say, 'I will pray and get over it. Jesus will save me.' You know all that business. Sorry, I am not belittling the word. Use the other words—Buddha or Krishna—it is the same thing with a different name, or the same symbol, the same content of the symbol. Symbols vary but they have the same content.

So is sorrow merely the ending of the actuality of certain memories? The actuality that created, that brought together those memories has ended and therefore I feel I am lost. I have lost my son. Is that sorrow or is it self-pity (we are not being harsh), concerned more with my own memories, pain, anxiety, than with the ending of somebody? Is that sorrow self-interest? Please go into it. I cultivate that memory; I am loyal to my son; I am loyal to my former wife, though I marry a new wife. I am very loyal to the remembrance of those things that have happened in the past. Is that sorrow? Then there is the sorrow of failure—you know the whole momentum of self-interest identifying itself with that word and shedding tears. And these tears have been shed by man and woman for a million years. And we are still crying. Those at war are crying, shot to pieces because of an idea that they must dominate, they must be different. The idea. Thought is destroying each one of us. And think of all the people who have cried before you.

So is there an end to sorrow? The word sorrow also implies passion. As long as there is self-interest identifying itself with those memories which are still there but of which the actuality has gone, that self-interest is part and parcel of the movement of sorrow. Can all that end? Where there is sorrow there cannot be love. So what is love? You know, we have entered into very, very serious subjects. It is not just something you play with for a Sunday or Wednesday morning. All this is something deeply serious. It is not galloping down the road. It is walking in the pathway slowly, watching things—watching, watching, watching, staying with things that disturb you, staying with things that please you, staying with things that are abstract—all the imaginings, all the things that the brain has put together, including God. It is the activity of thought. God didn't create us. We created God in our own image, which is—I won't go into this, it is so clear and simple.

To talk about love also implies death. Love, death and

creation. You understand? You can spend an hour on this because it is very, very serious. We are asking: what is creation? Not invention. Please differentiate between creation and invention. Invention is a new set of ideas, technological, psychological, scientific and so on. We are not talking about ideas. We are talking about very serious things: love, death and creation. This cannot be answered in five minutes. Forgive me. We will deal with it next Sunday. Not that I am inviting you. We will go into it, and also into what is religion, what is meditation and if there is something that is beyond all words, measure and thought—something not put together by thought, something that is inexpressible, infinite, timeless. We will go into all that. But one cannot come to it if there is fear, or lack of right relationships, you follow? Unless your brain is free from all that you cannot understand the other.

TALK FIVE
SUNDAY, JULY 21

This will be the last talk at Saanen. May we continue with what we were talking about last time we met here? We were saying among other things that this is not a lecture; a lecture is meant to inform, to instruct on a particular subject. Nor is it an entertainment. Entertainment means amusing yourself, going to a cinema, or to a ritual in a church or temple, or mosque. Nor is this a mere matter of intellectual, theoretical —what word shall we use?—psychological pursuit. Rather it is a philosophical pursuit, for philosophy means love of truth, not talking about what has already been talked about, and we are not discussing or concerned with what others have said. We are together, you and the speaker, as two human beings—not this large audience, but you as a person and the speaker are having a conversation together, about their life, about their problems, about all the travail of life—their confusion, their fears, their aspirations, their desires to achieve success, either in the business world or in the so-called religious, spiritual world; that is, success in reaching Nirvana, Heaven, or Enlightenment is the same as success in the business world. I hope we understand each other. A man who is successful in life, making pots of money, grows, expands, changes and continues in the line of success. There is not much difference between that person and the man who is seeking truth. Both are seeking success. One you call worldly, the other you call non-worldly, spiritual, religious. We are not dealing with either of those. We are concerned with you as a human being. You and the speaker are having a conversation together. He means together, though you are sitting there and the speaker unfortunately is sitting up here.

You and the speaker have been talking about relationship, between man and woman, boy and girl and so on. We have also been talking about fear, whether it is at all possible, living in the modern world, to be utterly free psychologically of all fear. We went into that very, very carefully. And we also talked about time, time by which we live, the cycle of time, which is the past being processed in the present and continuing in the future, the past being our whole background, racial, communal, religious, the experiences, the memories. All this is the background of all of us, whether we are born in the distant East or in Europe or in America. That background goes through changes, it is processed in the present and continues to the future. Human beings, you and another, are caught in this cycle. That has been going on for millions and millions of years. So the past going through the present, modifying itself, is the future. And that has been our evolution. Though biologically we have changed from a million years till now, psychologically, inwardly, subjectively we are more or less what we were a million years ago—barbarous, cruel, violent, competitive, egocentric. That is a fact. So the future is the present. Is this clear to you and to the speaker? The past modifying itself becomes the future, so the future is *now* unless there is a fundamental, psychological change. And that is what we are concerned about: whether it is possible for human beings, you and another, to bring about a psychological mutation, a total psychological revolution in oneself, knowing that if we are hurt now, wounded psychologically now, as most people are, the future hurt is *now*. Is that clear?

So is it possible for human beings, for you, to bring about a complete mutation? That mutation changes the brain cells themselves. That is, one has been going north all one's life, and some person comes along and says, 'Going north has no importance at all, no value, there is nothing there. Go east, or west, or south.' And because you listen, because you are concerned, because you are deliberate, you go east. At that very moment when you turn and go east there is a mutation in the brain cells because going north has become the pattern, the mode, and when you go east you break the pattern—right? It is as simple as that. But that requires listening, not merely to words, not merely with the hearing of the ear, but listening without any interpretation, without any comparison, listening directly, without bringing in all your traditions, your background, your interpretation. Then that very listening breaks down your conditioning.

And we also talked about seeing—seeing very, very clearly what is happening in the present world; wars and the most appalling things are going on everywhere. A million or two million years ago man killed with a club, then he invented an arrow. He thought that would stop all wars. Now you can vaporize millions and millions of people with one bomb.

We have progressed tremendously outwardly, technologically. The computer is probably going to take over all our thinking. It will do far better than we can in a second. I don't know if you have gone into this question, but you should. What is going to happen to the human brain when the computer can do almost anything that you can do, except, of course, sex? And it can't look at the stars and say, 'What a marvellous evening it is'; it can't possibly appreciate what beauty is. So what is going to happen to the human brain? Will it wither when the laser computer can take over thinking for you? It will save a lot of labour. Either we will turn to entertainment or turn in a totally different direction, because psychologically, inwardly, we can go limitlessly. The brain has an extraordinary capacity, each one's brain. Look what technology has done. But psychologically, subjectively, we remain what we are, year after year, century after century: conflict, struggle, pain, anxiety and all the rest of it. That's what we talked about in the last four talks.

And we also talked about thought: what is the nature of thinking, what is thinking? We went into that very carefully. All thought is memory, based on knowledge and knowledge is always limited, whether now or in the past or in the future. Knowledge is perpetually, eternally limited because it is based on experience which is also always limited.

This morning we ought to talk together, you and the speaker, not the whole audience (there is no whole audience, there is only you and the speaker)—we ought to talk together about love, death, what is religion, what is meditation, and if there is anything beyond all human endeavour—or is man the only measure? Is there something beyond the structure of thought, is there something that is timeless? That is what we have to be concerned with, you and the speaker, this morning. All right?

We live by sensation. We talked about that. Our whole structure is based on sensation—sexual, imaginative, romantic, fanciful and so on. And also, as we said, self-interest is the greatest corruption. And is sensation, that is, the stimulation of the senses—is sensation love? We are investigating this thing, you and the speaker, together. It is a long lane, you and the speaker are walking along together—not that he is ahead and you following, but together, in step; perhaps holding hands, friendly, neither dominating the other, not trying to impress each other. So you and the speaker are walking quietly, exploring, investigating, watching, listening, observing.

So we are asking each other: what is love? That word has been spoilt, spat upon, degraded, so we must be very alert to the abuse of that word. What is love? Is it mere sensation? I love you and I depend on you, you depend on me; perhaps I will sell you and you sell me; I use you, you use me. If the speaker says 'I love you' because you are a very big audience and feed my vanity and I feel happy, pleased, gratified—is that love? Is gratification, fulfilment, attachment, love? Is love put together by thought? You and the speaker are investigating together, so don't go to sleep on this lovely morning.

Is love sensation? Is love gratification? Is love fulfilment? Dependence? Is love desire? Please don't agree or disagree. We went into that—how we always approach things by either agreeing or disagreeing. Could we put aside altogether from our vocabulary, from our brain, 'I agree', or 'I don't agree' and just face facts as they are, not only in the world, but also in ourselves? That demands great honesty, the urgency of honesty. Can we do that this morning—face things as they are? Then we can begin to question, enquire, into what love is.

Is love desire? Previously in these talks, we went very deeply into the whole structure of desire. We haven't time to go into that again. Very briefly, desire is the result of sensation, and thought gives a shape, an image, to that sensation, and at that second when thought moulds the sensation, desire is born. So we are asking: is love desire? Is love thought? Please go into it. It is your life we are concerned with—our lives, our daily lives, not some spiritual life, not following some guru with his inanities, not putting on special robes, whether it be the robes of the Middle Ages or of the churches, or the robes of recent gurus. Is love merely the structure of thought? In our relationships with each other, man, woman, boy, girl and so on, when one says, 'I love you', is it dependence? One is fulfilling oneself in another and therefore in that relationship thought comes in, and then the thought creates the image, and that image we call love. So we are asking: is love—it is unfortunate to have to use that word—is love put together by thought? Can there be love when there is ambition, when we are competing with each other? Is there love when there is self-interest? Please don't merely listen to the speaker. Listen to yourself. Find out for yourself. When you discover something through what actually is, you can go very far, but if you merely depend on another, his words, his books, his reputation, it is meaningless. Throw away all that and look at oneself. One has to have passion. Passion can exist, as we said the other day, only when suffering ends. Passion without fanaticism, for with fanaticism it becomes terrorism. All the fanatical movements in the world have tremendous passion. Fanaticism breeds passion. That passion is not the passion which comes into being when there is the ending of sorrow. We went into that.

So we are asking: is love all this? Jealousy, which is in hate, anger, desire, pleasure and so on—is all that love? Dare we face all this? Are you and the speaker honest enough to discover for ourselves the perfume of that word?

From that we ought to consider what place death has in our life. Death, talking about it, is not morbid. It is part of our life. From childhood maybe till we actually die, there is always this dreadful fear of dying. Aren't you afraid of death? We have put it as far away as possible. So let us enquire together what is that extraordinary thing that we call death. It must be extraordinary. Let us enquire without any kind of romantic, comforting, belief in reincarnation or life after death. Reincarnation is a marvellously comforting idea. If one believes in it sincerely, deeply, as millions do, then it matters what you do now, what you are now, what your conduct, what your daily life is, because if there is a continuity, then next life you will have a better castle, a better refrigerator, better car, better wife, or husband. So could we put that comforting idea aside?

So what is death? First we must enquire into what is living—what do we mean by living? What do we mean by a good life? Is a good life having a lot of money, cars, changes of wives, or girls, or going from one guru to another and being caught up in his concentration camp? Please don't laugh, this is actually what is going on. Is a good life enjoyment, tremendous pleasure, excitement, a series of sensations, going to the office from morning till night for forty years? For God's sake, face all this. Working, working, and then dying. Is this what we call living—constant conflict, constant problems one after the other? In this life to which we cling, we have acquired a tremendous amount of information and knowledge about practically everything, and we cling to that knowledge. To those memories we have, we are deeply attached. All this is called living—pain, anxiety, uncertainty, and endless sorrow and conflict. And death comes through accident, old age, senility. That is a good word. What is senility? Why do you attribute it to old age? Why do you say, 'He is a senile old man'? I may be. Are you senile? Senility is forgetfulness, repeating, going back to the old memories, half alive—right? That is generally called senile. The speaker has asked this question very often of himself. Is senility an old-age problem? Or does senility begin when you are repeating, repeating, repeating? You follow? When you are traditional, continue to go to the churches, temples, mosques, repeat, repeat, repeat. Christians kneel, and the other fellow touches his forehead to the ground, and the Hindus prostrate. So senility can be at any age—right? Ask yourself that question.

Death can happen through old age, through an accident, through terrible pain, disease; and when it comes there is an end to all your continuity, to all your memories, to all your attachments, to your bank account, to your fame. So we ought to consider what is continuity and what is ending? May we go into that? What is it that continues and what is it that ends? Why are we so frightened of ending something, whether it be tradition, a habit, a memory, an experience? Not calculated ending, not ending something to achieve something else. You can't argue with death. There is a marvellous story of ancient India. I don't know if we have time for it because we have to talk about religion, meditation and whether there is something beyond all this human endeavour. All right, I will repeat that story very, very briefly.

A Brahmana—a Brahmana, you understand, a Brahmana of Ancient India—has collected a lot of things, cows and all the rest of it, and he decides to give them away, one by one. And his son comes to him and says, 'Why are you giving away all this?' He explains that when you collect a lot of things you must give them away and begin again. You understand the meaning of it, the significance? You collect and then give away everything that you have collected. (I am not asking you to do this.) So the boy keeps on asking that question. And the father gets angry with him and says, 'I will send you to Death if you ask me any more questions.' And the boy says, 'Why are you sending me to Death?' So when a Brahmana says he will do something, he must stick to it, he sends the boy to Death, and after talking to all the teachers, philosophers, gurus and all the rest of it, the boy arrives at the house of Death. (I am making it very, very brief.) And there he waits for three days. Follow the significance of all this, the subtlety of all this. He waits there for three days. Then Death comes along and apologizes for keeping him waiting because after all he is a Brahmana, so he apologizes and says, 'I will give you anything you want, riches, women, cows, property, anything you want.' And the boy says, 'But you will be at the end of it. You will always be at the end of everything.' And Death then talks about various things which the boy can't understand. It is really a marvellous story.

So let's come back to realities. What is death? Is time involved in it? Is time death? I am asking you, please consider it. Time, not only by the watch, by the sunset and sunrise, but also psychologically, inwardly. As long as there is self-interest, which is the wheel of time, there must be death. So is time related to death? Oh, come on, sirs. If there is no time, is there death? Please, this is real meditation, not all the phoney stuff. For us time is very important—time to succeed, time to grow in that success, and bring about a change in that success. Time means continuity. I have been, I am, I will be. There is this constant continuity in us, which is time. If there is no tomorrow—may I enter into all this? This is a dangerous subject. Please pay attention if you are interested in it, otherwise yawn and rest at ease. If there is no tomorrow, would you be afraid of death? If death is now, instant, there is no fear, is there? There is no time. You are capturing what I am saying? So, as long as thought functions in the field of time—which it is doing all day long—there is inevitably the feeling that life might end and therefore I am afraid. So time may be the enemy of death. Or time is death.

For instance, if the speaker is attached to his audience because out of that attachment he derives a great deal of excitement, sensation, importance, self-interest, or envy of a person who has a larger audience—if the speaker is attached, whether to an audience, to a book, to an experience, to a title, to a fame, then he is frightened of death. Attachment means time. I wonder if you understand all this? Attachment means time. So can I, can you, be completely free of attachment *now*? Not wait for death, but be free of that attachment completely *now*? Yes, sir. Face that fact.

So living is dying and therefore living is death. You understand what I am saying? Oh, come on, sirs. That is why one has to lay the foundation of understanding oneself not according to philosophers, psychiatrists, books and so on, but understand oneself, watch one's behaviour, one's conduct, one's habits—the racial, communal, traditional, personal accumulation we have collected through millennia upon millennia—know all that which is inside you. The knowledge, the awareness of that is not of time; it can be instant. And the mirror in which you see this is the relationship between you and another—to see in that relationship all the past, the present habits, the future; everything is there. To know how to look, how to observe, how to hear every word, every movement of thought, that requires great attention, watchfulness.

So death is not in the future. Death is now when there is no time, when there is no me becoming something, when there is no self-interest, no egotistic activity, which is all the process of time.

So living and dying are together always. You don't know the beauty of it. There is great energy in it. We live by energy. You take sufficient food, have the right diet and so on, and it gives a certain quality of energy. That energy is distorted when you smoke, drink and all the rest of it. The brain has extraordinary energy. And that extraordinary energy is required to find out for oneself, discover for oneself, and not be directed by another.

So now we are going to enquire into what is religion? We have talked about fear, we have talked about psychological wounds, not to carry them for the rest of one's life. We have talked about the significance of relationship. Nothing can exist on earth without relationship, and that relationship is destroyed when each one of us pursues his own ambition, his own greed, his own fulfilment, and so on. We have talked about fear. We went together into the question of thought, time, sorrow and the ending of sorrow. And we have talked this morning about death. Now we are capable of, alive to finding out, what religion is because we have got the energy. You understand? Because we have put all that human conflict and self-interest aside. If you have done that it gives you immense passion and energy, incalculable energy. So what is religion?

Is religion all the things that thought has put together? The rituals, the robes, the gurus, the perpetual repetition, prayers —is that religion? Or is it a big business concern? There is a temple in South India that makes a million dollars every third day. You understand what I am saying? Every third day that temple gathers one million dollars. And that is called religion. Is that religion? Going every Sunday morning to hear some preacher and repeating the ritual, is that religion? Or has religion nothing whatever to do with all that business? You can only ask this question when you are free from all that, not caught in the entanglement, in the performance, in the power, position, hierarchy of it all. Then only can you ask the question: what is religion? Is God created by thought, by fear? Is man the image of God? Or is God the image of man? Can one put all that aside in order to find out that which is not put together by thought, by sensation, by repetition, by rituals? Because all that is not religion—at least not for the speaker. All that has nothing to do with that which is sacred.

What then is truth? Is there such a thing as truth? Is there such a thing—an absolute, irrevocable truth, not dependent on time, environment, tradition, knowledge, or what the Buddha said, or what somebody else said? The word is not the truth. Therefore there is no personal worship. K is not important at all. We are seeking what is truth. If there is any. And if there is something that is beyond time. The ending of all time. They have said that meditation, a quick mind, is necessary to come upon this. We are going to go into it, if you will allow me.

What is meditation? The word means ponder over, according to the dictionary. To think over. It also has a different meaning in Sanskrit and in Latin, which is to measure. And to measure means comparison, of course. There is no measurement without comparison. So can the brain be free of measurement? Not measurement by the yard-stick, by kilometres, miles, but the measurement of becoming and not becoming, comparing, not comparing. You understand? Can the brain be free of this system of measurement? I need to measure to get a suit made. I need measurement to go from here to another place. Distance is measurement, time is measurement. Oh, come on. Can the brain be free of measurement? That is, comparison—have no comparison whatsoever so that the brain is totally free. This is real meditation. Is that possible, living in the modern world, making money, breeding children, sex, all the noise, the vulgarity, the circus that is going on in the name of religion? Can one be free of all that? Not in order to get something. To be free.

So meditation is not conscious meditation. You understand this? It cannot be conscious meditation, following a system, a guru—collective meditation, group meditation, single meditation, according to Zen or some other system. It cannot be a system because then you practise, practise, practise, and your brain gets more and more dull, more and more mechanical. So is there a meditation which has no direction, which is not conscious, deliberate? Find out.

That requires great energy, attention, passion. Then that very passion, energy, the intensity of it, is silence. Not contrived silence. It is the immense silence in which time, space is not. Then there is that which is unnamable, which is holy, eternal.

FIRST QUESTION AND ANSWER MEETING
TUESDAY, JULY 23

I have been told that there are so many people who are sad leaving, ending, Saanen. If one is sad it is about time that we left! And as has been announced, we are leaving. This is the last session at Saanen.

There are several questions that have been put. You can't possibly expect all those questions to be answered, there are too many. Probably it would take several days to answer them. The speaker has not seen these questions, he likes to come to them spontaneously, but they have been very carefully chosen.

Before going into these questions which you have put, may I ask you some questions? May I? Are you quite sure?

Why do you come here? That is a good question. What is the *raison d'être* or the cause of your coming? Is it curiosity? Is it the reputation the man, the speaker, has built for the last seventy years? Is it the beauty of this valley—the marvellous mountains, the flowing river and the great shadows and lovely hillside? What has brought you here? Is it that you are concerned with your daily life, the way you are living it, the problems that you have, probably of every kind, old age, death, sex—you know the whole invasion of problems our brain is so used to—and that you expect someone to tell you how to live, how to examine, what to do? Is that the reason you are here? Or is it that one wants to see what one actually is as we are sitting here, examine that very closely and see if we can go beyond it—is that the reason?

So, as you cannot possibly answer all those questions, I am asking you, the speaker is asking you, what is it all about? These gatherings have been going on in Saanen for twenty-five years. A great deal of our life. And, if one may ask the question of you, what remains at the end of it all, what is the content of our life? Is there any breaking of the pattern? Or is the pattern or mould being repeated over and over and over again? One's constant concentrated habits seem so difficult to break—the habit of thought, the habit of one's everyday life. When we look at all that after twenty-five years, is there a breaking of that pattern in which we live? Or do we just carry on day after day, adding a little more, taking away a little more, and at the end of one's existence feeling regret that one has not lived differently? Is this the process we are going through? I am asking the question: what is it all about? Our life. All the appalling things that are happening around us, far away from this lovely land? Where are we as individuals in this whole pattern of existence? What is the residue that remains in the sieve? What remains in us? Are we aware of what is happening to us in our daily thought, aware of every emotion, reaction, response, habit? Or is it just flowing by like a river?

Which would you like to answer first of these questions? [He reads them aloud.]

What do you mean by creation?
Various teachers, gurus, say that essentially they are giving the same teaching as you. What do you say?
What is guilt? One is desperate because the actions that caused the guilt can never be eradicated.
Can we start with the various teachers? Right? *Various teachers, gurus, say that essentially they are giving the same teaching as you. What do you say?*

I wonder why they compare themselves with the speaker. I wonder why they should even consider that what the speaker is saying is what they are also saying. Why do they say these things? I know this is a fact, that in India, Europe and America, various trumped-up gurus, various groups, say, 'We are also going towards the same thing, along the same river as you are.' This has been stated to me, to the speaker, personally, and we have discussed this matter with these gurus, with these local or foreign—what do you call them?—leaders. We have gone into this question.

First of all, why do they compare what they are saying with K? What is the intention behind it? Is it to ride on the same band wagon? Is it because they think they may not be 'quite quite' but by comparing themselves with K they might become 'quite quite'?

So in talking it over with some of them, we went into it. First of all I doubt what they are saying and I doubt the speaker's own experiences. There is a doubt, a disbelief, not saying, 'Yes, we are in the same boat.' So could we approach this question with doubt, with a certain sense of scepticism on both sides? There are those who say we are rowing the same boat on the same river; perhaps they are far ahead and the speaker is far behind, but it is still the same river. So in speaking with them, you doubt, question, demand, push further and further, deeper and deeper, and at the end of it, the speaker has heard many of them say, 'What you say is perfect, is the truth. You embody truth', and all that business. So they salute and go away saying, 'We have to deal with ordinary people and this is only for the élite.' I said, 'Double nonsense!' You understand?

So why do we at all compare—my guru is better than your guru? Why can't we look at things as they are? Questioning, doubting, asking, demanding, exploring, never saying our side is better than your side, or this side is better than that side, or that we are all doing the same thing. The other day I heard, 'What you are saying I am saying, what is the difference?' I said, 'None at all.' We use the same language, English or French, a little bit of Italian, but the content, the depth that lies behind the words may be quite different. We are so easily satisfied with explanations, with descriptions, with a sense of all the éclat, all the glory, all the paraphernalia. Our brains don't work very simply.

Have you ever watched, seen how your brain works? That is one of the questions I would like to ask you. Watched your brain in action as an outsider might watch it? You understand? Have you ever done it? Or is the brain carrying on with its old habits, beliefs, dogmas, rituals, business and so on—just mechanically carrying on? If I may ask, is your brain like that? Silence! Have you ever watched one thought chasing another thought, a series of associations, a series of memories, holding on to your own experience? The other day, in America, a person whom we have known for some time said that he lived according to his experience, what his experience has told him. His experience was real, actual, very deep, and that experience was all-important to him. And we said, 'Why don't you doubt your experience, it may not be actual? It may be imaginary; it may be romantic, sentimental and all the rest of it. Why don't you doubt that very thing you say: "My experience tells me"?' One has not seen that person again—do you understand?

So is it not necessary to be aware of all these things: why they compare, why they say we are all in the same boat? We may be in the same boat, probably we are, all of us. But why assume we are in the same boat? Can we not refuse to accept any guru, any leader, especially the speaker? Never accept anything psychologically except what we have watched in ourselves in our relationships, in our speech, the tone of voice, the words we use, all that. Can one all day, or some part of the day, be aware of all that? Then perhaps you won't need any guru, any leader, any book, including that of the speaker. Then, when one is really attentive, there is something totally different taking place.

May we go on to the next question? Good Lord! Guilt. I don't have to read the question. It is all rather mixed up here.

Why do we feel guilty? Many people do. It tortures their life. Then it becomes an enormous problem and that is the background of guilt for many, many people. Guilt in not believing, guilt in not being with the rest of the group. You know the feeling of guilt, not the word but the feeling behind that word—that we have done something wrong and feel remorseful, anxious, and therefore frightened, uncertain. This guilt is a very distorting factor in our life. This is obvious. So why do we have this feeling? Is it that we have not done something which is correct, which is not pragmatic, which is against what our environment has put together? The guilt of a man or woman who feels they haven't supported the war of their own country. You know the various forms of guilt and the causes of it. We are asking: why does this feeling exist? Is it because we are not responsible, not demanding excellence of ourselves?

Now, just a minute, the speaker is asking, is it that we are lazy, indolent, inattentive and therefore slightly irresponsible? And facing that irresponsibility we feel guilty? Suppose I have followed somebody, my guru, who has indulged in all kinds of things, sex and so on, and I have done as he does, then he changes his mind, he becomes old and says, 'No more', and his disciples say, 'No more.' One has done all these things in order to follow that guru and then the guru says, 'No more', and I feel I shouldn't have done those things, I have been wrong. You follow? The whole issue of guilt. How do we deal with it? That is more important.

So let's find out what to do about it, shall we? Not investigate the causes of it, we know those. I have done something which is not proper, which is not correct, which is not true and I realize later that that reaction has been unfortunate, causing damage to myself and unhappiness to others and I feel guilty. So what shall we do when we have guilt? How would you deal with it? What is your approach to it? How do you come near the problem? Is it that you want it resolved, that you want it wiped away so that your brain is no longer caught in it? How do you approach it—with the desire to resolve it, to be free of it? How you approach a problem is very important, isn't it? If you have a direction for that problem, it must be solved this way or that way. Or if you have a motive, then that motive directs the issue. So do we approach a problem like guilt without any motive? You understand my question? Or do we always approach a problem with a motive? I wonder, are we meeting this thing together? Is it possible to approach a problem without any sense of the background knowledge which is motive, and look at it as though for the first time? Can we do that?

So, there are two things involved: how you approach a problem and what is a problem. You have problems, don't you, many, many of them? Why? Not that we are condemning the problem or saying it must be solved this way or that way; we are questioning the problem itself, the word, and the content of that word, an issue, something which you have to answer, whether it is a business problem, family problem, sexual problem, spiritual problem—sorry, 'spiritual' should be in quotes—problems as to what leader to follow. Why do we have problems?

First let's examine the word problem. According to the dictionary, a problem means something thrown at you, something propelled against you, a challenge, a thing that you have to answer. Something thrown at you. And we call that a problem. Why does our brain have problems? May we go into it a little bit? Please don't accept anything the speaker says, *anything*. But let's examine it together. When you send a child to school, he has to learn to read and write. He has never read or written before, so writing and reading become a problem to him. And as he grows up his brain is being trained to problems. Obviously. The whole process of learning is a problem and so the brain is conditioned in problems. This is a fact. My wife becomes a problem, how to live, what to do, and so on and so on. Our brain, your brain, is conditioned, educated to live with problems. This is a fact, not an invention by the speaker. It is so. So our whole life becomes a problem. Can we look at this as a fact, not as an idea, or a theory, but as a fact and see what we can do—whether the brain can be free to solve problems, not approach them with a mind that is already crowded with problems? You understand my question? No? I have been to school where I am not interested in anything the teacher is saying. I am looking out of the window, enjoying myself; he bangs me on the head. I come to, and he says, 'Write.' I say, 'Good Lord, I must learn', and it becomes a problem to me. My whole education—I am not against education but I am pointing out—my whole education becomes a tremendous problem. So the brain from childhood is conditioned to live with problems—right?

Now, our question is: is it possible to be free of problems and then attack problems, for I cannot resolve them unless the brain is free. If it is not free, in the solution of one problem other problems are created. So the speaker is asking: can we be free of problems first—uncondition the brain which has been educated to live with problems? Is it clear? At last.

Now let's proceed. Is it possible to be free and then tackle problems? How do you answer that question? Do you say it is possible or do you say it is impossible? When you say it is possible or impossible you have already blocked yourself. You have already closed the doors. You have prevented yourself from investigating, going into the question.

So here is the question again: is it possible to free the brain from the conditioning of its education? The speaker is going into it not to convince you of anything but just to show you. You are not to do anything. Just listen to what he is saying, not accepting or denying, just looking, listening. The brain is conditioned to this whole culture of problems. That is a nice word—culture of problems. And is the conditioned brain different from the observer? Is the brain, my brain, different from me who is analysing, looking, tearing, examining, accepting, not accepting—is that observer, the person who says, 'I am looking at it', any different from the brain? It is a very simple question, don't complicate it. Is anger, greed, envy, different from me? Or am I anger? Anger is me. Greed is me. The quality is me. There is no difference. But culture, education, has made us separate them. There is envy: if I say I am different from it, that I must control it, or indulge in it, there is conflict. I don't know if you are following all this? Is envy me? Is violence me? Violence is not something different from me; me is violent. Do you see this? Once one realizes this fact that there is no difference between the quality and me, then a totally different movement is taking place. There is no conflict. You understand? There is no conflict.

As long as there is separation there is conflict in me.

Now I realize this, that I *am* the quality. I am violence. I, the me, is greedy, envious, jealous and all the rest of it, so I have abolished altogether this division in me. I am that. I am that quality. So, can my brain remain with that fact, stay with that fact? Can my brain, which is so active, so alive, thinking, watching, listening, trying, making efforts—can that brain stay with the fact that I am that? Stay with it, not run away, not try to control, because the moment you control there is a controller and the controlled, therefore it becomes effort. Please, I am being very simple. If you really grasp this truth, this fact, you eliminate effort altogether. Effort means contradiction. Effort means, I am different from that. Can you see the actual fact, not the idea but the actuality that you are your quality, your anger, your envy, your jealousy, your hate, your uncertainty, your confusion—that you are that? Not acknowledge it verbally or verbally agree, then we don't meet each other, but actually see this fact and stay with it. Can you? When you stay with it, what is implied in that? Attention—right? No movement away from it. Just staying with it. If you have acute pain you can't stay with it, but if you stay with it psychologically, inwardly say yes, it is so—which means no movement away from the fact—then the essence is no conflict, then you have broken the pattern of the brain. The pattern says, 'I must do something. What is the right thing to do? Who will tell me the right thing to do? I must go to a psychiatrist'—you know all that stuff that takes place. When once you see the fact, it is like holding a jewel, marvellously carved; you are looking at it, seeing all the inside, outside, how it is put together, the platinum, the gold, the diamonds. You watch it because you are the jewel, you are the centre of this most intricate, subtle jewel which you are. The moment one sees the fact the whole thing is different.

So guilt—sorry I have gone away from it. We had to. Guilt. It is not a problem, you understand now. It is a fact. It is not something to be resolved, something to be got over. You feel guilty about something you have done; this is a fact, and you stay with it. When you stay with it, it begins—please listen—it begins to flower and wither away. You understand, sir? Like a flower, if you keep on pulling it up to see if the roots are working properly, it will never bloom, but once you see the fact, which is the seed, and then stay with it, it shows itself fully. All the implications of guilt, all the implications of its subtlety, where it hides, is like a flower blooming. And if you let it bloom, not act, not say, 'I must do or must not do', then it begins to wither away and die. Please understand this. With every issue you can do that. About God, about anything. That is insight, not merely remembrance, adding. Is this clear? If you discover it, you see that it is so, then psychologically it is an enormous factor that frees you from all the past and present struggles and effort.

Now for the first question: *What do you mean by creation?*

Shall we go into that? It is a rather complex question. I will read it again. *What do you mean by creation?* What does the speaker mean? I would like to put that question to you.

A lot of people talk about creation—the astro-physicists and the theoretical philosophers. God created and so on.

This is a very serious question which the ancient Hindus and the ancient Hebrews have put, not merely recent scientists. This has been a tremendous issue that they want to understand. May we go into this?

What is creation? When you ask that question you must also ask the question, what is invention? Is invention creation? To invent something new, is that creation? Careful please, don't agree or disagree, just look at it. Invention is based on knowledge—right? It is based on somebody else's previous experiments; all those experiments are knowledge in the present and you add to it. This is so. The man who invented the jet knew first all about the propeller and the internal combustion machinery; then from that knowledge he got an idea. I may be putting it incorrectly, or exaggeratedly, but this is so: from a great deal of knowledge, a new inspiration comes, and that inspiration is an invention. So we are adding all the time. And is that creation—something which is based on knowledge and the consequences of knowledge? Or has creation nothing to do with knowledge? Is creation a series of inventions in the universe? Obviously when they look at Mars, Mercury, Venus, Saturn and go beyond, they know what Venus is made of—various gases and so on and so on and so on—but what they have translated as gases is not Venus. You understand? Come on, sirs. The word Venus is not Venus. The gases constituting Venus are not that beauty which you see early in the morning or late in the evening.

So we are asking, is invention totally different from creation? Which means that creation has nothing whatever to do with knowledge. You are going to find this rather difficult. If you don't mind, if you are not too tired, if you still have the energy to investigate, we will go into it. Don't accept what the speaker is saying, that would be terrible. It would destroy you. Don't merely say, yes, yes, yes. It would destroy your brain, as it has been destroyed by others. The speaker has no intention of destroying your brain, or adding to the already damaged brain. So he says have scepticism, question, don't accept or deny, just find out. We know what invention is—at least to the speaker it is very clear. That doesn't mean it is clear to you. We are asking, what is creation?

Is creation related to man's endeavour? Is it related to all experiences? To the duration of time? Please examine all this. Which means, is it related to war, to killing, to business, to all the memories that man has accumulated, acquired, gathered? If it is, then it is still part of knowledge. Therefore it cannot be creation. Right? So what is creation? Is it related —please listen, just listen, don't do anything about it—is it related to love? That is, love is not hate, jealousy, anxiety, uncertainty, the love of your wife, which is the love of the image you have built about her, or of your husband or girl friend, or the image you have built about your guru for whom you have great devotion, or the image of a temple, mosque, or church. So we are asking: is love necessary for creation? Or is love, which is also compassion, creation? And is creation or love related to death? You understand all these questions? I am sorry to ask, do you understand—I withdraw that. Just listen.

So is love free from all the human beings who have given

specific meaning to that word? Free from all that. Is love related to death? And is love compassion and death? Is all that creation? Can there be creation without death? That is, ending. Ending all knowledge—Vedanta. You have heard that word, I am sure. The word Vedanta means the end of knowledge—the end of knowledge which is death, which means no time, timeless, which is love. You understand? Sorry, I won't repeat that. Stupid of me to repeat!

So love, death. Love means compassion. Love, compassion mean supreme intelligence, not the intelligence of books and scholars and experience. That is necessary at a certain level but there is the quintessence of all intelligence when there is love, compassion. There cannot be compassion and love without death, which is the ending of everything. Then there is creation. That is, the universe, not according to the astro-physicists and scientists, is supreme order. Of course. Sunrise and sunset. Supreme order. And that order can only exist when there is supreme intelligence. And that intelligence cannot exist without compassion and love and death. This is not a process of meditation but deep, profound enquiry. Enquiry with great silence, not 'I am investigating'. Great silence, great space. That which is essentially love and compassion and death is that intelligence which is creation. Creation is there when the other two are there, death and love. Everything else is invention.

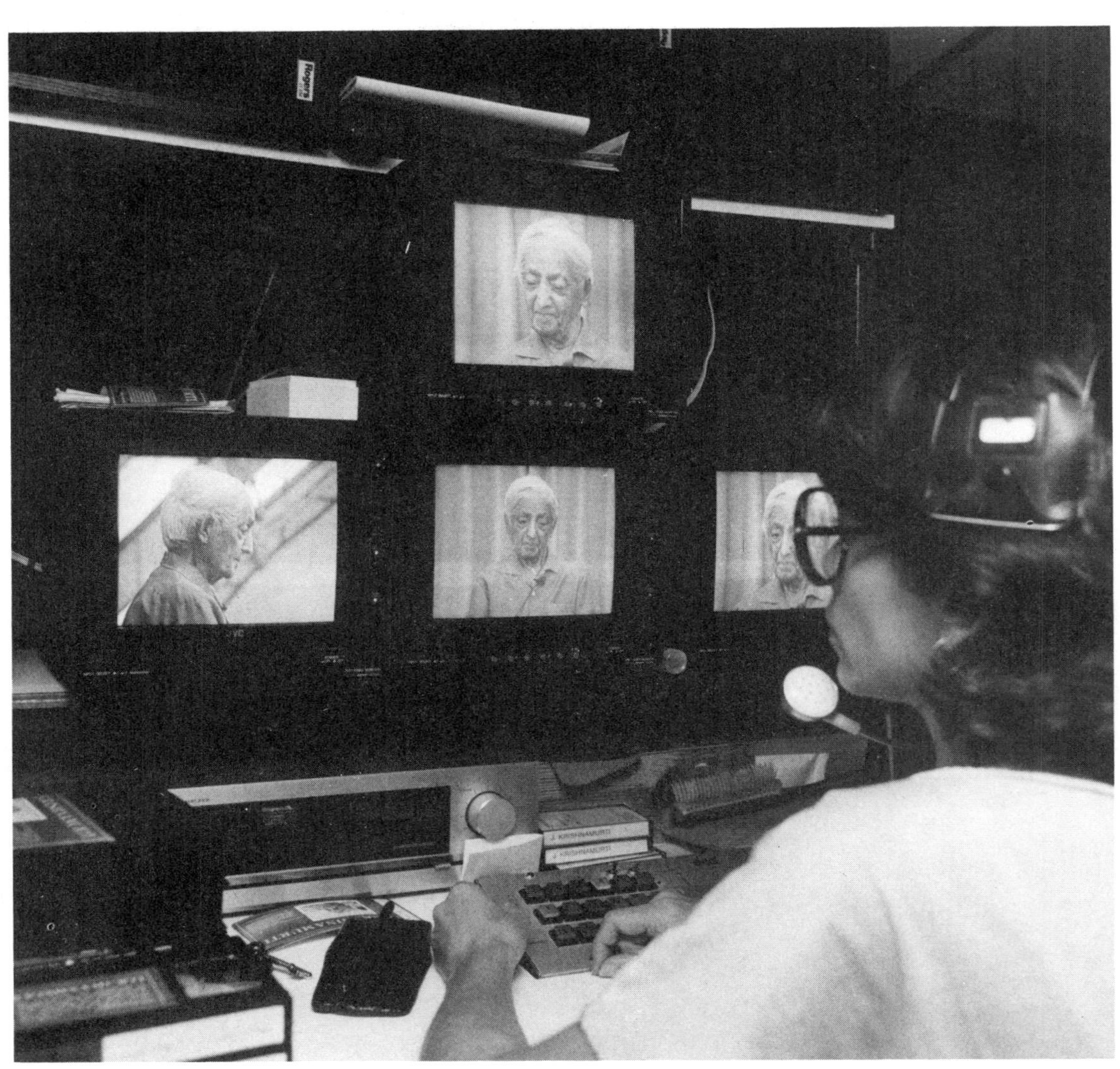
Rogers
J. KRISHNAMURTI
J. KRISHNAMURTI

SECOND QUESTION AND ANSWER MEETING
WEDNESDAY, JULY 24

Let's forget for the moment the questions. We will come back to them.

What is happening to all of us, living in this world, which is quite terrible? If you have travelled at all you will see the dangers—airport explosions, terrorists, and all the rest of it. When you look at it all, how do you face the world? We may be old, but the coming generation, children, grandchildren, and so on, what is going to happen to them? Do you consider that at all? What is the future of the coming generation of which you are a part? How do we educate them, what is the purpose of education? Presumably we are all educated. You have been to school, college, university, if you are lucky, or we have been educating ourselves by looking at all these events that are taking place in the world and learning from them. But that learning is very limited, very small, narrow. And if one has children and grandchildren, how does one treat them? What is our response? Aren't we concerned about them at all? I believe there are about 500,000 children who run away from home in America, end up in New York, prostitution and all that—do you understand what it all means? In a country like this, part of the rest of the world, there is no poverty, no slums, there are literally no people starving. There are slums in America, England, France, and all those starving people in India and Asia; it is quite appalling, degrading. And when we look at ourselves and the future generation, what is going to happen? Is that same pattern going to be repeated? The same callousness? The irresponsibility of being trained in an army to kill thousands and thousands, and be killed? What is our responsibility? Or don't you want to think about all that at all? Are we only concerned with our own pleasure, with our own problems, with our own self-centred egotistic activity?

This is really a very serious question, frightening, agonizing. When we look at all this, what do we do? Do we have proper schools? What place has knowledge in all this, whether it be theoretical or physical knowledge? What relationship have we to it all? The tortures. Every country has indulged in torturing other human beings. My mother may be tortured, my son, for some information, for some nationalistic, communistic or democratic reason. Do we shed tears? Or not being able to do anything about it, do we become cynical, bitter and throw in our hands?

So, we have to consider all these things, not merely our own progress, our own happiness, our own self-centred activities.

May we go on now with the questions? Maybe that will be more pleasant, less challenging, less demanding on our energies and the capacities of the brain. The brain has extraordinary capacity and energy if you have watched all the progress in the fields of medicine and surgery, technology, computers—tremendous advances, incalculable advances.

And it is going on and on. In other directions the brain is very limited, and that limitation is being used by the technological world. We are being exploited ruthlessly. The Communists still have their concentration camps, and there are not only the concentration camps of tyrannies but also the concentration camps of the gurus. You don't mind my saying that? And the concentration camps of all the monks in the world. This is really a tremendous problem.

When one understands something must one act on this understanding, or does the understanding act of itself? Right? Question clear?

Now what do we mean by understanding? We use that word so easily. So we must investigate, explore the meaning of the word. We are discussing, exploring together, the speaker is not answering the question. Together we are looking into the question. We are together investigating, digging into the meaning of words first, according to the dictionary, which is the common usage of the language. What do we mean by understanding, to understand something? To understand oneself, to understand how the computer, which is so marvellous, works, to understand the whole surgical process. What do we mean by that word? Is it purely intellectual, which is a quick communication between two people, or half a dozen people or a hundred people, a comprehension of the meaning of the word, quickly translated to the brain, and the intellect saying, 'Yes, I understand'? That is, I have a problem, I have reasoned it out, I have come to a conclusion and I understand it. Or I understand how to dismantle a car and so on. So is understanding merely an intellectual affair, a theoretical affair about which I can talk endlessly, adding more ideas to it and thinking I am enlarging, growing? In that understanding is there any emotional quality? Is there something that says, 'That is not quite, quite, quite, you must add more to it'?

There is the intellect, there is emotion, there is action—right? Emotions exist naturally—one hopes—but when those emotions have become romantic, sentimental and very, very superficial, they must be recognized by the brain, therefore they are part of the brain—part of the sensation of feeling, sensation of imagination, of looking at a mountain, the beauty and the silence and the dignity and the majesty of it, and putting it on a canvas, or writing a poem about it. All that is still part of the activity of the brain. So is the intellect, which says, 'I understand', the capacity to discern, to distinguish, to determine and take action and therefore dominating everything else?

So we are asking, is understanding a whole movement, not an act of the brain only, an act of the intellect only? Do you understand my question? We will now have to examine what is action? What is it that one has to do? What determines action? What brings about action? What do we mean by action? To act. To do. Is that action based on an ideal, or on a theory, or a conclusion, dialectical or imaginative? That is, I act on an idea—right? So what is an idea? Why do we have so many ideas? We are investigating the word idea, not whether it is right or wrong. The scientists, the physicists and the theoretical philosophers want ideas, otherwise they feel lost. They want new ideas all the time. So we must examine what we mean by an idea. There is a fact. There is a clock there. It says ten to eleven, and that is a fact. And there are non-facts. The non-facts are totally away from the fact. Distance. And so there is the fact and the idea about the fact, and we pursue the idea, not the investigation into the fact. An idea becomes far more important than the fact. The Socialists, the Communists and others, left, right, centre, all have ideas, theories, conclusions, and they try to fit man into those ideas. And to make them fit they torture them, they say, 'You can't do this, you can't do that.' So to them ideas become far more important than the human which is the fact.

So, are we, each one of us, always moving away from the fact and pursuing an idea and acting according to that idea which probably has nothing to do with the fact? So what do we mean by acting? If you act according to your past memories, experiences, or some future ideological conclusion, that action, based on the past or on the future, is not an act. Are we making this clear? If we act according to certain memories, conclusions, experiences, knowledge, then we are acting from the past. The word act means do, not according to the past or according to the future. So the question is—go into this, it is very serious—is there an action which is not based on time? Don't be puzzled. Can one grasp the significance, the content, the deep meaning of the past, how the past, modified, projects itself into the future, and how if one acts according to the past or according to some future concept it is not action; it is merely memory, having come to certain conclusions, acting. So it is always caught in the field of time, in the cycle of time—right?

Now we are asking, is there an action which is not based on time? Think it out, sirs. Think it out, don't wait for me, for the speaker, to explain; think it out. It is a very simple question, but has tremendous meaning behind it. That is, I have always acted according to my tradition. The tradition may be one day old, or five thousand years old. You know what tradition means, *tradere* hand over. So my parents, grandparents, a thousand parents, have handed over certain traditions, the consequences of their thought, their feeling, gradually seeping through various generations; and I am that, part of that. That is my background and I act according to that. Or I reject all that, saying, 'How stupid', and look to the future; I must do this, I must not do it, according to some leader whom I follow. And I call both these action. But the speaker asks, is there an action which is not based on these two, an action which is not the process of the time? Sorry, you have to use your brains.

What is one to do when one is asked that question: is there an action which is not caught in the wheel of time? How does one's brain react to that question—the brain which has been conditioned, shaped according to the past and the future, that is, caught in the field of time, in the network of time? The brain withdraws for the moment, is not able to answer; it says, 'It is too much trouble, for goodness sake leave me alone. I am used to this pattern, it has brought its misery, suffering, but also there is the other compensating side to it. Don't ask these questions which are so difficult.' They are not difficult. The word difficult makes it difficult. So I won't use that word. But I have to find out if there is an action which is not of time. May I go into it? Do you want me to go into it?

Action is related to love, not to memory. Memory, remembering the images, is not love; it is sensation through which I act, and sensation is not love. Therefore what is the relationship of love to action? You follow? Is love memory? We have met together, we have slept together, we have done all kind of things together, walked up the mountain, down the valley, round the hills, been companions, held hands, quarrelled—and that is called affection, love, but most of it is based on sensation, the image, and attachment. Without attachment I am lost, I feel terribly lonely. Feeling lonely, I am desperate, become bitter and all the rest of it. Is all that love? Obviously it is not. We went into it. So what is the relationship between love and action? Go on, sir. If love is in the field of time, then it is not love. So love is action—I wonder if you get this? There is not love first and action later. For the speaker—don't accept it—for the speaker there is no division between the perception, the quality of that love and action. When there is that quality it is action. It is not an intellectual process of determination or choice. It is an action of immediate perception.

Now we must go on. Yesterday we only answered three questions and there are many more of them.

You have said many things about violence. Would you allow one of your friends to be attacked in front of you?

It is a good old question. What would you do if your sister was attacked in front of you? It is the same question. What would you do—you? Beat him up? Shoot him? Karate? You know what that word karate means? It has been explained to me. No self. No me. Not the military art of defending yourself. So what would you do? Find out, sir. You are there, with your wife or husband or your girl friend, and somebody comes along and is violent towards your wife or husband. What would you do instinctively? You would attack, wouldn't you? Naturally. You would hit him. If you knew karate, or some kind of yoga tricks, you would trip him up. So this question is put to me, to the speaker—right? We know the normal reaction of people, violence. If you are violent I am going to be violent. If you are angry with me I am going to be doubly angry with you. If you call me an idiot, I say you are a greater one. And so on and so on. This question is put to me, to the speaker. This has been an old question, but I treat all questions as something new. What should I do? Are you waiting for me?

If I have lived a violent life all my life then my response would naturally be violent. But if I have lived as I have without violence, not only physical violence but psychological violence, which is aggression, competition, comparison, imitation, conformity (that is all part of violence)—lived as K has lived—then when my friend, or my sister, or my wife, is attacked I would act as I have lived.

A simple answer. You are not puzzled over this, are you? No.

Another question: *What is intelligence?*

What is intelligence? What do you think is intelligence? One meaning of that word, if you looked into a good etymological dictionary, is *interlegere*, to read between the lines. Another meaning is to gather information of every kind and to discern among the various kinds of information what is correct. That depends on choice, on one's education, on one's way of life and so on. Then there is the intelligence of the body, if you let it alone. The body is an extraordinary instrument—how all the nerves are connected to the brain, how the liver works, the heart. From the moment it is born until it dies the heart keeps on beating. It is an extraordinary machine. If you have seen some of the photographs on television where they show the body, it is amazing what nature has done through a million or two million years. But we destroy the native intelligence of the body by doing all kinds of extravagant things—drinking, drugs, sex (though sex has its place)—you know the whole issue of it, ambition, greed, fighting, struggling, a tremendous strain on the body, heart failure: all that affects the brain, the nerves, the organism, and therefore the physical, biological instrument is gradually destroyed; it gradually withers and loses its vitality, its energy. If one leaves it alone, it looks after itself, you don't have to do a thing, except for a person like K who is ninety years old and so has to be a little careful.

Then there is the intelligence of a clever physician, or a technologist, or a man who puts very, very complex machinery together, and the thousands of people who get together to send a rocket to the moon—that requires great intelligence and co-operation, a certain type of intelligence. There is also the very cunning, calculated, intelligence which has put together all the rituals of the world—the temples, the mosques, the churches—controlling people through their apostolic succession, sorry if you are a Catholic, forget what I am saying! (There is also in India a Sanskrit word for it, this handing down.) It demands great intelligence to control people, to make them believe in something that may or may not exist, to have faith, to be baptized. It is all very clever if you have watched it, very intelligent. The Communists are doing it; they have their god, Lenin, and after him Stalin, all the way down to the present gentlemen. So it is the same movement. All that is partially very intelligent. And the scientists, the theoretical physicists, are also partially very intelligent.

Then what is a holistic intelligence? You understand? Intelligence which is whole, which is not fragmented. I am very intelligent in one direction, but in other directions I am dull. There is partial intelligence in various phases of life. But we are asking, is there an intelligence which is complete, which is not fragmented? Are you going to find out? Or am I going to find out and tell you? Please, am I going to answer that question or are you going to answer it?

Is there an intelligence which is incorruptible, not based on circumstances, not pragmatic, not self-centred and therefore broken up, not whole? Is there an intelligence which is impeccable, which has no holes in it, which covers the whole field of man? To enquire into it the brain must be completely free of any conclusion, any kind of attachment, any kind of self-centred movement, self-interest, and therefore a brain that is totally free from fear, from sorrow. When there is the end of sorrow there is passion behind it. The word sorrow etymologically has a deeper meaning than merely shedding tears, pain and grief and anxiety. Passion is not *for* something. Passion is *per se*, for itself. A belief may invoke passion in me, or devotion to a symbol, a community, something I imagine, but all that is still very limited. So one has to discover, one has to come upon, this passion which is neither lust nor has any motive. Is there such passion? There is such passion when there is an end to sorrow. When there is an end to sorrow there is love and compassion. And when there is compassion, not for this or that, but compassion, then that compassion has its own supreme quintessence of intelligence. That is, it is neither of time, nor does it belong to any theories, to any technologies, to anybody; that intelligence is not personal or universal, nor the words round it.

Is there any benefit to the human being in physical illness?

Is there any benefit, reward, profit, to the human being in physical illness? In being ill? Now I put that question to you.

I am sure most of us have been ill at one time or another, either mentally ill, that is an illness of the brain, which is neurotic, psychopathic and so on, or physically ill, some organ not functioning properly. Now just listen: what is the difference between illness and health? What is health? What is it to be extraordinarily well? The question is: is there any profit, benefit, from illness? What do you think? To that question the speaker would say there is—sorry! When you are ill, what are your reactions, responses? The desire when one is ill is to avoid pain, to take a pill quickly, or immediately go to a doctor, and he tells you what to do. You want to get over it quickly because you may lose your job, etc. etc.

But if you are not afraid of illness, illness has quite a

different meaning. The speaker, if I may be slightly personal, was paralysed for a month in Kashmir for various reasons; they over-dosed the poor chap with antibiotics, and a few days later he was paralysed for a month. I thought that was final. I thought, there it is. The speaker wasn't frightened. He said, 'All right, I'm paralysed for the rest of my life.' This actually happened. I am not exaggerating. They carried me, washed me and all the rest of it, for a whole month. You know what that means? Fortunately you don't. But if I had struggled against it and said, 'What stupid doctors. I am anti-antibiotics', it would have made it worse and I would have learnt nothing from it; it wouldn't have cleansed my body, it wouldn't have benefited me. The speaker has several times been very, very ill. I am not going into that. But if one is not afraid to remain with it, to stay with it, does not immediately rush to a doctor or to a pill, physical illness has a certain natural profit, benefit. You may have to take a pill later, but go at it slowly, patiently, observing what your reactions are, why there is this craze to be healthy, to have no pain, which makes you resist the illness. This self-interest may be one of the factors of illness. It may be the true reason for illness. Do you understand all this? Clear? Right.

Why do you differentiate between the brain and the mind?

I am afraid this has to be the last question. There are several left over but this has to be the last one.

First of all what is the brain? Remember that we are not professionals; we are ordinary people who are not brain specialists. Though the speaker has talked to brain specialists, he is *not*, not underlined, a brain specialist. So we are asking each other what is the brain, not the physical biological structure of the brain, I don't know anything about all that. But what is this thing we live with which is in operation in our daily life, not superior consciousness or lower consciousness? You know that game. That is what the gurus play at. They help you to bring down the higher consciousness to lower consciousness, or through meditation, through following them, through repeating certain practices, to reach the higher consciousness. We are not doing all that kind of thing. We will come presently to what is consciousness. You don't mind going into all this?

What then is the function, the daily function of our brain—your brain, not my brain, your brain, the human brain, whether you live in Switzerland, America, Russia or the Far East—what goes on in our daily life which is the exercise of the brain, exercise of thought, exercise of choice, exercise of decision and action?

Wherever we live the activity of the brain plays a great role in our life. So what is this brain? We are amateurs, learning. Look at our own brain. Action and reaction. Sensation. Conditioned from the past—I am a Hindu, you are a Christian, I am a Buddhist, you are a Muslim and so on; I belong to this country and you belong to that country; I believe very strongly; I have come to certain conclusions, I stick to them; my prejudices and opinions are strong, and I am attached, I want to fulfil, I want to become something—you follow? That is our daily routine, and much more: the anguish of anxiety, tremendously depressing loneliness, and escaping from that loneliness through television, books, rituals, temple, church, mosque, God. Conflict. Conflict. Conflict. That is what the brain is caught up in all the time. This is not exaggerated. We are facing facts. It is so. The brain is the centre of all this—the memories, the nervous responses, the likes and dislikes—it is the very centre of all our existence, emotionally, imaginatively, art, science, knowledge. So that brain is very, very limited and yet it is extraordinarily capable. Technologically it has done incredible things, unimaginable fifty years ago. All that is the activity of the conditioned brain. And living within that conditioning—religious, political, business and so on—is very limited, concerned with oneself, self-serving. This is obvious. The brain says, 'I am materialistic', and it says also, 'No, no, I am better than that. There is a soul.' To use the Sanskrit word, 'There is an Atman', and so on and so on. So consciousness is all that—right? People have written books and books about consciousness, professionals and non-professionals, but we are not professionals, we are dealing with what is.

Consciousness is its content. What it contains makes consciousness. It contains anxiety, belief, faith, bitterness, loneliness, jealousy, hate, violence—you know, all the qualities, the experiences of human beings. That is, consciousness is not yours because every human being on this earth, whether the poorest, most ignorant, degraded, or the most highly sophisticated, educated, has these problems. They may put on robes and crowns and all that circus, but remove all that and they are like you and me. So we share the consciousness of every human being in the world. I know you won't accept this, it doesn't matter: this is a fact because you suffer and that villager in India who lives on one meal a day also suffers, not in the way you suffer, but it is still suffering. Your memories may be different from another's, but it is still memory. Your experience may be different, but it is still experience. So your consciousness is not yours. It is psychologically the consciousness of the entire humanity. You may be tall, you may be fair, I may be black, I may be purple, but still that consciousness is common to all of us—psychologically.

So you are the entire humanity. You know what that means? If you accept it as an idea then you move away from the fact, from the truth of it, from the reality, the substance of it. When there is that reality, truth, that you are the rest of mankind, then the whole movement of life changes. You will not kill another, for then you are killing yourself. There was an American General—oh, I have forgotten his name. He was going to war and he faces the enemy. And he reports to the boss, 'We have met the enemy. We are the enemy.' You understand? We have met the enemy across the field but we are the enemy, the enemy is us.

So when there is this truth that you are the entire humanity, sleep with it, go into it, feel your way into it, don't deny it or accept it, but as the river flows, go into it. You will see what a deep transformation takes place, which is not intellectual, imaginative, sentimental or romantic. In that there is a tremendous sense of compassion, love. And when there is that, you act according to supreme intelligence.

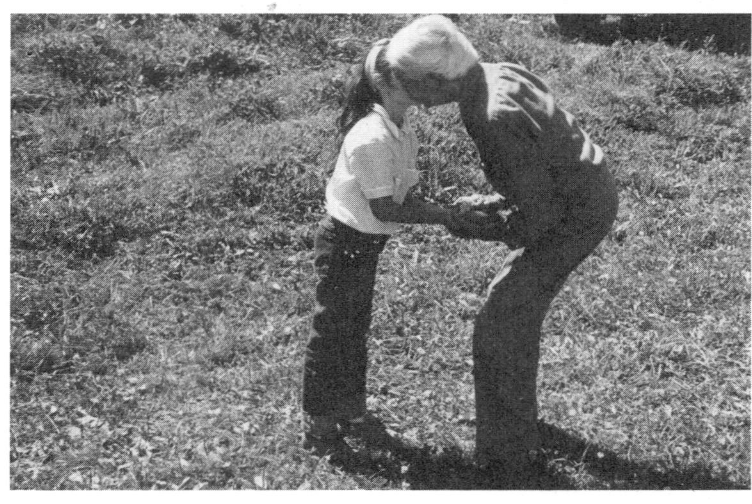

THIRD QUESTION AND ANSWER MEETING THURSDAY, JULY 25

There are too many questions to be able to answer all of them, but some of them have been chosen. I repeat, the speaker has not seen them.

Before we go into those questions may I comment on something? People have been talking a great deal about art, about what is art. I believe the root meaning of that word is to put everything in its proper place. Can we talk a little bit about that first?

What do you think is the greatest art, the supreme art? Is it the art of listening, hearing, seeing, observing, perceiving and learning? Please, together we are investigating into this question, not the speaker talking to himself.

Let us begin with the art of hearing. We not only hear with the ears—words conveyed, vibrated to the brain; surely it is much more than that. Do we ever listen to anybody? Do you listen to your wife or husband, or your girl friend, really listen to what they are conveying, trying to say? Or do you translate what is being said into your own terminology, compare it with what you already know, judging, evaluating, agreeing, disagreeing? Is that listening? The speaker is talking now, unfortunately; are you listening, actually paying attention to the meaning of words, to the content of the words, not translating, comparing, judging, agreeing, disagreeing —but just listening? Are you doing that now? Isn't it one of the most important things, how we listen to another? That other may be wearing too strong a perfume and you are repelled by it, or you like it, and this like and dislike of a perfume, or other factors, may prevent you from listening to what the other person has to say.

If you have gone into this question rather deeply you will find it is one of the most difficult things to listen to another, completely. Are you doing it now? Or are you fidgety and so on?

So there is an art of hearing, of listening—right? And there is an art of seeing—seeing things as they are. When you look at a tree, do you translate it immediately into words and say, 'Tree'? Or do you look at it, perceive it, see the shape of it, see the beauty of the light on a leaf, see the quality of that tree? It is not man-made fortunately; it is there. So do we see ourselves as we are, without condemnation, without judgement, evaluation and so on, just see what we are, our reactions and responses, our prejudices, opinions—just see them, not to do anything about it but just observe them. Can we do that?

So there is an art of seeing things as they are, without naming, without being caught in the network of words, without the whole operation of thinking interfering with perception. That is a great art.

And also there is an art of learning, isn't there? What do we mean by learning? Generally learning is understood to mean memorizing, accumulating, storing up to use skilfully or not, learning a language, reading, writing, communicating and so on. The modern computers can do most of that better than we can. They are extraordinarily rapid. So what is the difference between us and the computer? The computer must be programmed. We also have been programmed in various ways: tradition, so-called culture, knowledge. And we have also been programmed to be Hindu, Buddhist, Christian, Communist and all the rest of it. Is this all there is to learning? We are questioning. We are not saying that it is not. It is necessary to learn how to drive a car; to learn a language, and so on. But we are asking, is learning something much more? Are we together in this? Don't just look at me, please—the person is not very interesting. We are asking something, which is: is learning merely memorizing? For if that is all, then the computer can do better than us. But isn't learning something much more? Learning means constantly learning, not accumulating, not gathering in what one has seen, what one has observed, heard, learnt and storing it up.

Learning means, to the speaker, a constant observation, listening, moving, never taking a stand, never taking a position, never going back to memory and letting memory act. That is a great art.

Then there is the art of discipline. That word comes from disciple, one who learns from someone else, not necessarily from the teacher, from the guru—they are generally rather stupid—but to discipline oneself according to a pattern, like a soldier, like a monk, like a person who wants to be very austere and disciplines his body: the whole process of control, direction, obedience, subservience and training. To me, to the speaker, discipline is a terrible thing. But if there is acute hearing, not only by the ear, but also deep listening to yourself, to everything that is happening around you, listening to the birds, to the river, to the forest, to the mountain, and observing the minutest insect on the floor, if you have good eyes to see it—all that constitutes a form of living which in itself becomes the discipline, there is constant movement.

I will go back to the question. Phew! It is pretty hot here! We have had most marvellous days, three weeks of it, lovely mornings, beautiful evenings, long shadows and the deep blue valleys and the clear blue sky and the snow. We have had a marvellous three weeks. A whole summer has never been like this. So the mountains, the valleys, the trees and the river, tell us goodbye. Can we go on with our questions?

I see that thought is responsible for my confusion. And yet in going into it, more thought is generated and there is no end to it. Please comment on this.

Thought is associated with other thoughts—right? There is no single thought. It is a series of movements which we call thinking. I think about my shoes, then how to keep them clean; I polish them (which I do). So thought by itself cannot exist—that is, one thought without all the associations in connection with it. And thinking is the very life of us. That is so obvious. You couldn't be there and the speaker couldn't be here if we hadn't thought about it. We thought about it because there have been previous associations—reputation, books and all the 'bla', and you come here and I come, the speaker comes. So there is no single thought by itself. This is important to uncover. Thought is always in relation to something else; and in pursuing one thought other thoughts arise. The speaker is polishing his shoes and looks out of the window and he sees those mountains and he is off! And he has to come back and polish his shoes. I want to concentrate on something and the thought shoots off in another direction. I pull it back and try to concentrate. This goes on all the time from childhood until we die.

And the more I think about thought, the more thought there is: 'I shouldn't think along those lines, I must think rightly, is there right thinking, is there wrong thinking, is there purposeful thinking, what is the purpose of my life', and so on? The whole process of thinking begins and there is no end to it. It has done the most extraordinary things. Technologically it has done the most appalling things, terrifying things. It has built all the rituals of every religion, and it has tortured human beings. It has expelled people from one part of the world to another, and so on and so on. Thought, whether Eastern or Western, is still thinking. It is not Eastern thinking and Western thinking, two separate things. Because thought is the thread—right? We are together?

So the question is: is there an end to thought—not your way of thinking, or my way of thinking, or saying we are all thinking together, we are all moving in the same direction? We are asking whether thought can ever stop. Which is, is there an end to time? Thinking is the result of knowledge, memory. To acquire knowledge, one needs time. Even the computer, which is so extraordinary, has to be given a split second before it gallops out what it wants to say. So when we are asking whether thought can ever end, we are also asking whether there is a stop to time. It is a rather interesting question if you go into it.

Time, what does that mean to us, not only psychologically but outwardly—sunset, sunrise, learning a language and so on and so on? You need time to go from here to there. Even the fastest train or aeroplane needs time to get here or there. So . . . please follow this—as long as there is a distance between 'what is' and 'what might be', 'what I am' and 'what I will be'—it may be a very short distance or centuries of distance—that distance can only be covered by time. So time implies evolution—right? You plant the seed in the earth, it takes a whole season to mature, grow, or a thousand years to become a full tree. Everything that grows or becomes needs time. Everything. So time and thought are not two separate movements. They are one solid movement. And we are asking whether thought and time have an end, a stop? How will you find out? This has been one of the problems confronting the human being from the beginning of man. This movement of time is a circle; time is a bondage. The hope, I hope, involves time. So man has asked not if there is timelessness but rather if there is an end to time. You understand the difference?

This is really a very serious question. We are not enquiring into the timeless. We are enquiring whether time, which is thought, has a stop. Now how will you discover that? Through analysis? Through so-called intuition? That word intuition, which has been used so much, may be most dangerous, it may be our hidden desire. It may be our deeply-rooted motive of which we are not aware. It may be the prompting of our tendency, our own idiosyncrasy, our own particular accumulation of knowledge. So we are asking, if you put all that aside, has time a stop? And we asked, how will you find out? You, not the speaker or anybody else, because what others say has no importance.

So, we have to enquire very, very deeply into the nature of time, which we did during the last few talks. We also went very deeply into the nature of thinking. Can all that come to an end? Or is it a gradual process? If it is a gradual process, the very gradualness is time, so it cannot be gradual—right? It cannot be 'eventually'. It cannot be next weekend or tomorrow, or a few minutes later. It cannot be the next second either. All that allows time. If one really grasps all this, deeply comprehends the nature of thought, the nature of time, discipline, the art of living—stay with it quietly, not cover it up by all kinds of movements, but stay with it—then there is a glimpse of its nature, an insight into it, which is not related to memory, to anything. Find out! The speaker can easily say, yes there is. That would be too childish. Unless we experiment—not just say yes, yes, or agree—unless we actually investigate, experiment, push it, go into it deeply, we can't come upon a strange sense of timelessness. The second question says: *Please speak further on time and death.*

We have talked a great deal about time, thought, and what relationship time has to death. What relationship has thought, thinking, to this extraordinary thing called death? If one is frightened of death then one will never see the dignity, the beauty and the depth of death. Fear is caused by thought and time. We have been into that very carefully. Fear doesn't exist by itself. Fear exists where there is a demand for security, not only biological, physical, security but much more. Human beings apparently insist, demand, require, to be psychologically secure.

So we have to enquire into security, that is being safe, protected. Security means protection—right? I have to protect that which gives me security, whether it is security of position, security of power, security of a great many possessions. To have millions in the bank gives you a great sense of security. To possess a good chalet gives you security. Security also implies having a companion who will stand by you, who will help you, who will comfort you, who will give you what you want and what she wants. So in the family we seek security. In the community we seek it. In the nation, in the tribe, and that very tribalism, nationalism, prevent that security because there is war, one tribe killing another tribe, one group destroying another group. So physically it's becoming more and more difficult to be secure. The terrorists might come into this tent and blow us all up.

We not only need physical security but also psychological security. Psychological security is the greatest demand. But we are asking: is there psychological security at all? Please ask yourself this really very, very serious question: is there inwardly, subjectively, inside the skin as it were, any security at all? I can rely on you as an audience and you can rely on me as the speaker. If the speaker seeks security in you and has nobody to talk to, then he feels terribly insecure. So is there psychological security at all?

The world is changing constantly from day to day, it is in

tremendous flux. It is so obvious. Physically one needs a little security to sit here, talk together, but that is gradually being restricted. You cannot do that in Communist countries. So one recognizes the fact that psychologically there is no security. That is the truth; there is no psychological security. I can believe, I can have faith, but you come along and tear it to pieces. The more I strengthen myself in belief the more that belief can be torn to pieces. I may have faith in something, in a symbol, in a person, but that can be pulled to pieces by argument, logic. So there is no psychological security at all. Though we have sought it, though we have tried to fulfil ourselves, done everything to be secure psychologically, at the end of it there is death.

There is death. And death is the most extraordinary thing. Putting an end to long continuity. In that continuity we hope to find security because the brain can only function excellently when it is completely secure—secure from terrorism, secure in a belief, secure in knowledge and so on and so on. All that comes to an end when there is death. I may have hope for the next life and all that stuff, but it is really the ending of a long continuity. I have identified myself with that continuity. That continuity is me. And death says, 'Sorry old boy that is the end.' And one is not frightened of death, really not frightened, for you are living constantly with death—that is, constantly ending. Not continuing and ending, but ending every day that which you have gathered, that which you have memorized, that which you have experienced.

Time gives us hope, thought gives us comfort, thought assures us a continuity, and we say, 'Well, in the next life . . .'

But if I don't end this silliness now, the stupidity, the illusions, and all the rest of it, they will be there in the next life—if there is a next life.

So time, thought, give continuity, and we cling to that continuity and therefore there is fear. And fear destroys love. Love, compassion and death. They are not separate movements.

So we are asking: can we live with death, and can thought and time have a stop? They are all related. Don't separate time, thought and death. It is all one thing.

Is it not violence and corruption to have physical security while others are starving?

Who is asking this question? Please, the speaker is asking you, who has asked this question? Is it the man with physical security considering the poor, the starving, or is it the starving who are asking this question? If you and I are comfortable we can ask this question. If you and I are really very poor would we ask this question? You see, there are so many social reformers in the world, the do-gooders. I won't go into it now because we haven't time for it. Look at it carefully. Are they fulfilling themselves in social work, doing something for the poor? This question has been put to the speaker when he is in India—what are you doing for the poor? They are starving, you seem to be well fed, what do you do? So I am asking, who puts this question? The speaker is not avoiding the question. He has been brought up in poverty. Is it then the speaker when he was young, living in poverty, asking this question?

There is poverty in the world; there are slums, appalling

conditions. (There are no slums in Switzerland apparently. Thank God!) There are slums, ghettos, the very, very, very poor, one meal a day and all that. What do we do about it? That is really the question, isn't it? You may be wealthy, I may not be so wealthy, but the question is: what do we human beings, seeing all this, do about it? What is our responsibility? Are we concerned—please, we are not avoiding the question—are we concerned with poverty? Poverty. What does that mean? Physical poverty? Or psychological poverty? You understand? Being poor, psychologically, in the sense that you may have a lot of knowledge about the psyche but are still poor. The analyst is poor, and he is trying to correct the other person who is also poor.

So what is poverty? To be poor, not to be sophisticated, to be ignorant. So what is ignorance? Is it the lack of reading a book, of writing, having only one meal a day, one cloth a day? Or does poverty begin first psychologically? If I am rich inwardly I can do something. If I myself am poor inwardly, poverty means nothing outside.

So we have to understand not only what poverty is, but all that is involved in it—sympathy, generosity. If you have one shirt, you give it. Once the speaker was walking in the rain in India and a little boy came up and said, 'Give me your shirt.' I said, 'All right.' So I gave it to him. Then he said, 'Give me your undershirt.' I said, 'Just a minute. Come with me to the house. You can have anything you like, food, clothes, anything you like, within limits of course.' So he came with me, holding my hand; he was very poor, dirty. It was pouring and we walked together to the house. I left him, and went upstairs to get some clothes for him. And the boy went round the house, looking into every cupboard, all over the place. The person with whom the speaker was staying caught him and said, 'What are you doing in this part of the house?' 'He asked me to come in,' he said. 'But he didn't ask you to come upstairs and look into everything. So why are you doing it?' And the boy got rather frightened and said, 'My father is a robber.' He was casing the house.

So we have to deal with poverty not only externally but also inwardly. Probably there would be no poverty in the world if all the nations got together and said we must solve this problem. They could. But nationalities divide them, communities divide them, religious beliefs divide them. So the whole world is opposed to the kind of action that puts aside all our nationalities, beliefs, religions and really helps by working all together to solve this problem of external poverty. Nobody will do this. We have talked to politicians, to higher people, but they are not interested. So begin with ourselves.

How can our limited brain grasp the unlimited, which is beauty and truth? What is the ground of compassion and intelligence and can it really come upon each one of us? Right? Question clear?

How can our limited brain grasp the unlimited? It cannot, because it is limited. Can we grasp the significance, the depth, of the quality of the brain and recognize the fact—the fact not the idea—that our brains are limited by knowledge, by specialities, by particular disciplines, by belonging to a group, a nationality, and all the rest of it, which is basically self-interest, camouflaged, hidden, by all kinds of things—robes, crowns, rituals? Essentially, this limitation comes into being when there is self-interest. That is so obvious. When I am concerned with my own happiness, with my own fulfilment, with my own success, that very self-interest limits the quality of the brain and the energy of the brain—not, as we explained, that the speaker is a specialist in brains though he has talked to several professional people about it.

That brain, for millions of years, has evolved in time, death, and thought. Evolution means, does it not, a whole series of time events? To put all the religious rituals together needs time. So the brain has been conditioned, limited by its own volition, seeking its own security, keeping to its own backyard, saying, 'I believe', 'I don't believe', 'I agree', 'I don't agree', 'This is my opinion', 'This is my judgement' —self-interest. Whether it is in the hierarchy of religion, or among the various noted politicians, or the man who seeks power through money, or the professor with his tremendous scholastic knowledge, or the gurus, all of whom are talking about goodness, peace, and all the rest of it, it is part of self-interest. Face all this.

So our brain has become very, very, very small—not in its shape or its size, but we have reduced the quality of it which has immense capacity. Immense. Technologically, it has improved, and it also has immense capacity to go inwardly very, very, very deeply, but self-interest limits it. To discover for oneself where self-interest is hidden, is very subtle. It may hide behind an illusion, in neuroticism, in make-believe, in some family name. Uncover every stone, every blade of grass to find out. Either you take time to find out, which again becomes a bondage, or you see the thing, grasp it, have an insight into it instantly. When you have a complete insight it covers the whole field.

So the questioner says, how can the brain, which is conditioned, grasp the unlimited, which is beauty, love and truth? What is the ground of compassion and intelligence, and can it come upon us—upon each one of us? Are you inviting compassion? Are you inviting intelligence? Are you inviting beauty, love and truth? Are you trying to grasp it? I am asking you. Are you trying to grasp what is the quality of intelligence, compassion, the immense sense of beauty, the perfume of love and that truth which has no path to it? Is that what you are grasping—wanting to find out the ground upon which it dwells? Can the limited brain grasp this? You cannot possibly grasp it, hold it, though you do all kinds of meditation, fast, torture yourself, become terribly austere, having one cloth, or one robe. The rich cannot come to the truth, neither can the poor, nor the people who have taken a vow of celibacy, of silence, of austerity. All that is determined by thought, put together sequentially by thought; it is all the cultivation of deliberate thought, of deliberate intent. As a person said to the speaker, 'Give me twelve years and I'll make you see God.'

So, as the brain is limited, do whatever you will, sit cross-legged, lotus posture, go off into a trance, meditate, stand on your head, or on one leg—whatever you do, you will never come upon it. Compassion doesn't come to it.

Therefore one must understand what love is. Love is not sensation. Love is not pleasure, desire, fulfilment. Love is not jealousy, hatred. Love has sympathy, generosity and tact, but these qualities are not love. To understand that, to come to that, requires a great sense and appreciation of beauty. Not the beauty of a woman or of a man, or a cinema star. Beauty is not in the mountain, in the skies, in the valleys, or in the flowing river. Beauty exists only where there is love. And beauty, love is compassion. There is no ground for compassion; it doesn't stay at your convenience. That beauty, love, truth is the highest form of intelligence. When there is that intelligence there is action, clarity, a tremendous sense of dignity. It is something unimaginable. And that which is not to be imagined, or the unlimited, cannot be put into words. It can be described; philosophers have described it, but the philosophers who have described it are not that which they have described.

So to come upon this great sense, there must be the absence of the me, the ego, egocentric activity, the becoming. There must be a great silence in one. Silence means emptiness of everything. In that there is vast space. Where there is vast space there is immense energy, not self-interested energy—unlimited energy.